# Synopses of
# SHAKESPEARE'S
# COMPLETE PLAYS

*By*
*Lewis M. Magill*
*Nelson A. Ault*

## About the Book

1. Thumbnail sketches of the main characters are included in the listings which precede each play.

2. Scenes as well as acts are clearly designated throughout the summaries of the plays.

3. The Synopses will be of inestimable value to students preparing for examinations; or for students wishing to preview the plots of the plays before reading the original text.

4. Helpful background material precedes each play and a general introduction discusses quartos and folios, the chronology of the plays, and interesting sidelights on Shakespeare's development.

## About the Authors

Both authors are Associate Professors of English at the State College of Washington.

# Synopses of
# SHAKESPEARE'S
# COMPLETE PLAYS

*By*

LEWIS M. MAGILL
NELSON A. AULT

*Department of English*
*State College of Washington*

1962

LITTLEFIELD, ADAMS & CO.
PATERSON, NEW JERSEY

# PREFACE

In preparing these synopses, we have tried to remain conscious of an unexceptionable axiom: the best synopsis in the world cannot do justice to an artistic masterpiece. We have handled Shakespeare's achievements carefully; and, except for some necessary, and we hope helpful, interpretations following the listing of certain characters, we have added nothing to Shakespeare's own texts. Insofar as Shakespeare's plots contributed to the finished product, they are here for inspection.

In particular we believe that we have employed a helpful device in using scene as well as act divisions. The reader should find it quite easy to locate almost any event in the plays. He will notice, however, that not always do the scenes appear in their chronological sequence. The reason for this should be obvious: Although the lack of scenery on the Elizabethan stage allowed the playwright to leave one group of characters for another, that one for a third, and the third for the original group in a succession of short scenes, we have refused to sacrifice the plot continuity to mere sequence of scenes. The early comedies particularly do not lend themselves to any other treatment.

Undergraduate Shakespeare students should be able to use these synopses both as aids in reading the plays and for review. But the usefulness of the synopses is not confined to undergraduates. Most graduate students, as well, can find them of inestimable value in preparing for specific and general examinations.

We have, of course, tried to keep in mind the needs of the general reading public as well as those of students. While this book is not a handbook in any accepted sense, it may be used as a guide through the Shakespearian canon for those who wish to reread the plays, as well as for those who are coming to them for the first time.

We have omitted a number of sections which would be of only limited value to most readers. Our controlling principle has been to concentrate on the plots of the plays, never sacrificing completeness of plot summary for non-essentials. We have included comprehensive but brief treatments of the folio-quarto problem, of the approximate order of the plays, and of Shakespeare's development. To do more would be to beg the question. Millions of words have been written—in handbooks, introductions, and studies—about Shakespeare's life, Shakespeare's theatre, Shakespeare's "quotable quotes," and Shakespeare's development. Many of these are readily available. Many, too, are of doubtful value, for some of these matters are highly conjectural. For example, except for a few illuminating dates, next to nothing is *known* about the life of Shakespeare; and it seems unlikely that much more will be discovered. Why worry about it? We have the plays themselves, for which we should be eternally grateful.

In conclusion, we should like to repeat this word of caution: Synopses are not the works themselves, and they should be used invariably in connection with the plays.

L.M.M.
N.A.A.

# TABLE OF CONTENTS

# INTRODUCTION

## SHAKESPEARE'S QUARTOS AND FOLIOS

Many beginning readers of Shakespeare are puzzled by the frequent references in the standard editions of his works to Shakespeare's *quartos* and *folios*. The terms themselves refer to book sizes. A folio is a book in which the pages are formed by folding a sheet of paper once. Thus, each sheet of printing stock is used to make two leaves. To form a quarto, the sheet is folded again. This procedure makes a smaller page, four leaves to the sheet. Another folding produces an octavo, still smaller than the quarto. More folding of the stock sheet results in progressively smaller pages.

Printers of Shakespeare's day used the quarto edition for printing relatively short works. Thus, if a Shakespearean play was printed as a separate work, the book was put together as a quarto. If, however, several plays were printed together as a collection, the printer made a folio, since a lengthy quarto volume would be bulky and hard to bind. When a Shakespeare editor refers to a *quarto* or to a play printed *in quarto,* he means a play that has been printed as a separate work. When he speaks of a *folio edition* or simply *folio,* he means a collected edition of several plays.

A number of Shakespeare's plays were printed separately in quarto before the first collected edition of his work appeared. Two of the quartos differ so greatly from the later collected editions that scholars cannot agree whether or not they are really the same plays. Some scholars believe that a quarto play called *The True Contention* is a different version of Part II of *Henry VI* as it appears in the first collected edition, and that *The True Tragedy of Richard, Duke of York* is a quarto version of Part III of *Henry VI*.

If these two doubtful quartos are accepted, nineteen of Shakespeare's plays appeared in quarto previous to the first collected edition: Part II of *Henry VI* (1594); Part III of *Henry VI* (1595); *Richard II* (1597); *Richard III* (1597); *Romeo and Juliet* (1597); *Love's Labour's Lost* (1598); Part I of *Henry IV* (1598); *Much Ado About Nothing* (1600); *Midsummer Night's Dream* (1600); *Merchant of Venice* (1600); Part II of *Henry IV* (1600); *Henry V* (1600); *Titus Andronicus* (1600); *Merry Wives of Windsor* (1602); *Hamlet* (1603); *King Lear* (1608); *Troilus and Cressida* (1609); *Pericles* (1609); and *Othello* (1622). One reason for noting the quartos is that they serve as an index to the popularity of the various plays in their own day. A play which was published in quarto was probably popular; otherwise there would have been no demand for a printed edition.

Many editors further classify the quartos as *duplicates, variants,* and *doublets.* These terms can be simply explained. Duplicate quartos are those from which the first collected edition was made (that is, they were "duplicated" in the collected edition). A variant quarto means any quarto which differs from the version included in the first collected edition. A doublet quarto is a play published in quarto twice, each edition varying from the other. There are two doublet quartos, *Romeo and Juliet,* and *Hamlet.*

Besides these designations, some of the variant quartos are called *bad* quartos. A group of first quartos including *The Merry Wives of Windsor, Henry V, Romeo and Juliet, Hamlet, Pericles;* and, of course, *The True Contention* and *The True Tragedy of Richard of York* are so designated. In the bad quartos, scenes are omitted and altered, speeches are paraphrased and garbled, verse is written for prose and prose for verse, characters are left out. It was once thought that the bad quartos were earlier versions of the plays which were eventually worked over by the author before being reprinted. Modern scholars believe, however, that the bad quartos were actually published from "pirated" or stolen manuscripts printed without consent of the theatrical companies which owned the plays.

The first collected edition of Shakespeare was published by Heming and Condell in 1623. It is usually called the "First Folio Edition" or simply the "First Folio." As a text, it is hardly more reliable than the quartos, though it is more uniform. There is often very little choice, so far as reliability is concerned, between the variant quartos and the folio. In the case of the doublet quartos, the second quarto edition offers a better text than the first folio. The real value of the first folio lies in the fact that it contains the only early text of eighteen plays. In all it contains thirty-six plays, twenty of which had not been previously printed.

Three other folio editions of Shakespeare were prepared during the seventeenth century—in 1632, 1663-4, and 1685. Each of these draws heavily upon the previous folios; hence, they tend to perpetuate errors in the text. The fourth folio (1695) includes many corrections and more nearly approximates a modern text than do the others. Next to the first folio of 1623, this edition is the most important folio to students of Shakespeare.

## THE CHRONOLOGY OF THE PLAYS

In the First Folio (1623), the editors arranged the plays in a purely arbitrary manner—(1) comedies, (2) histories, and (3) tragedies—with no attempt to follow chronological order. For instance, *The Tempest,* a play which all modern scholars accept as one of Shakespeare's latest efforts, is the first entry in the Folio. For many years, various editors of Shakespeare have consequently attempted by various methods to establish the dates of the plays. These methods fall roughly into three categories: examination of external, external-internal, and internal evidence.

External evidence consists chiefly of references to the various plays in extant books and pamphlets written by Shakespeare's contemporaries. For example, in Francis Meres' *Palladis Tamia* (1598) may be found a partial list of Shakespeare's plays to that date. Meres mentions *The Two Gentlemen of Verona, The Comedy of Errors, Love's Labour's Lost, Love's Labour's Won* (variously identified), *The Merchant of Venice, Richard II, Richard III, Henry IV, King John, Titus Andronicus,* and *Romeo and Juliet.* Obviously, these dramas must have been played before 1598. Although Meres' list is perhaps the most nearly complete of the contemporary references of Shakespeare's plays, it does not stand alone.

External-internal evidence rests primarily on references to contemporary events within the plays themselves. Perhaps the most interesting of these is the reference in *Henry V*, V, Prologue, ll .29-34, to the anticipated return of the Earl of Essex to England from his Irish campaign. Shakespeare traditionally was an Essex partisan, probably because the Earl of Southampton, Shakespeare's patron, belonged to the Essex faction; but not even partiality for Essex could lead Shakespeare to write these lines after the complete failure of the Irish junket. The date of the play, consequently, must lie between March, 1599, when Essex set out for Ireland, and September, 1599, when he returned to England. This piece of evidence is the most definite that can be found in the Shakespearean canon, but it is not the only one.

Internal evidence rests on an examination of Shakespeare's style, prosody, subject-matter, and dramatic technique. It is perhaps the most valuable (and, in a sense, the trickiest) of the three types of evidence. For instance, one of the internal tests in dating a play consists in determining the number of rhymed lines it contains. In the early plays, Shakespeare was consciously experimenting with metrics and language. The earliest plays almost invariably contain a number of interspersed lyrics (note, for example, that some of the speeches in *Romeo and Juliet* fall into the sonnet pattern); they also are filled with puns and other plays on words. Shakespeare, furthermore, in the early tragedies was imitating Marlowe's blank verse, with its oratorical, turgid qualities and its end-stopped lines; in fact, some early scholars were so impressed with the similarity of the blank verse in *Richard III* to that employed by Marlowe in his tragedies that they believe *Richard III* to be a collaboration of Shakespeare and Marlowe. As Shakespeare developed, his blank verse became a more supple and dramatic instrument of expression: for example, in the later tragedies, he creates stops at various points within the lines rather than invariably at the ends of lines, and even distributes one line among several speakers.

Although there is no general agreement among all scholars as to the exact date of several of the plays, a chronological list looks something like the following:

1588 - *Love's Labour's Lost.*

1589 - *The Comedy of Errors.*

1590 - *The Two Gentlemen of Verona.*

1591 - *I Henry VI, II Henry VI, III Henry VI.*

1592 - *Titus Andronicus.*

1593 - *Richard III.*

1594 - *Romeo and Juliet, The Taming of the Shrew, A Midsummer Night's Dream.*

1595 - *King John, Richard II.*

1596 - *The Merchant of Venice.*

1597 - *I Henry IV, II Henry IV.*

1598 - *The Merry Wives of Windsor, Much Ado About Nothing.*

1599 - *Henry V, Julius Caesar.*

1600 - *As You Like It, Twelfth Night.*

1601 - *All's Well That Ends Well, Hamlet (?), Troilus and Cressida.*

1604 - *Measure for Measure, Othello.*

1605 - *King Lear.*

1606 - *Macbeth.*

1607 - *Antony and Cleopatra, Timon of Athens.*

1608 - *Pericles, Coriolanus.*

1610 - *Cymbeline.*

1611 - *The Winter's Tale, The Tempest.*

1612 - *Henry VIII.*

## SHAKESPEARE'S DEVELOPMENT

A bare chronology of the Shakespearean canon is a sterile thing without some consideration of the growth of Shakespeare's genius. One of the notions popularized by such early nineteenth-century critics as Coleridge was that Shakespeare was a natural genius "warbling his woodnotes wild." These critics fell into what George Bernard Shaw called "bardolatry"; that is, they implied that Shakespeare was a demigod who could do no wrong. Modern scholarship, on the other hand, has established that in Stratford Shakespeare received a classical education which compares favorably, except in scientific fields, with a modern college education. In other words, not only was Shakespeare a trained man; but with a few exceptions, like Jonson, Chapman, and the University Wits, he was as well educated as any of his contemporaries.

The modern view, therefore, is one which regards him as a man of his time, doing what his contemporary playwrights were doing, and doing it immeasurably better. In fact, this view enhances, rather than detracts from his genius.

One of the first acts of the modern historical critics was to divide Shakespeare's producing years into four periods. Men like Edward Dowden called these periods by imaginative names which implied that the character of the plays was determined by events in Shakespeare's life; in other words, they assumed that Shakespeare wrote primarily for himself as an emotional catharsis. Most of the later scholars, however, have come to the conclusion that Shakespeare wrote particular kinds of plays at various times in his career in obedience to the exigencies of the box-office. Although perhaps one should not disregard the possible subjectivity of some of the plays, more than likely Shakespeare was primarily interested in satisfying the demands of play-goers.

One cannot ignore, however, the fact that Shakespeare's writing career can profitably be studied by periods. The first of these is usually called the period of experimentation (1588-1594), during which Shakespeare was learning his craft. Most of the plays are contrived comedies, deriving to a considerable extent from the Roman comic writers, Plautus and Terence. They are filled with lyric poetry and experiments with language. The early tragedies, like *Titus Andronicus* and *Richard III,* contain stiff Marlovian blank verse, and plotwise rest on the revenge motif inherited from Seneca and his imitators: blood, violent action, lust, and revenge are the basic elements of these tragedies.

Shakespeare's second period (1594-1600) includes the so-called joyous comedies, in which there are occasionally some serious overtones, but whose mood, in general, is a happy one. During this time also Shakespeare rose to the mastery of both the chronicle play and the historical tragedy. In the earlier chronicle plays Shakespeare followed Marlowe's lead quite closely; during the second period, he interspersed comic prose passages (Falstaff, Pistol, etc.) between sections written in a supple blank verse which Shakespeare had made more nearly his own instrument of expression.

The third period (1601-1608) includes all the great tragedies and the so-called bitter comedies. Most critics will agree that in *Hamlet, King Lear, Othello, Macbeth,* and perhaps *Antony and Cleopatra,* Shakespeare reached the summit of his achievement. He is aware of the power of evil in the world, and, in these tragedies, treats of it as one controlling force in the lives of men. Invariably, however, after moral values have been turned topsy-turvy during the course of these tragedies, the plays end in a world that, for the time being at least, has been washed clean of evil. Poetically these tragedies are unsurpassed in the literature of the world: the blank verse with which Shakespeare has been experimenting becomes in these plays a flexible, sonorous, and sometimes a startling instrument of great power. The characters in the tragedies are living, breathing entities, so much so that certain psychologists have been led into a blind alley by their attempts to psychoanalyze Hamlet and some of the others.

The bitter comedies do not succeed so well. In *Measure for Measure, All's Well That Ends Well,* and *Troilus and Cressida,* Shakespeare treats the same power of evil as in the tragedies; but in wrenching the plots to provide a fortunate outcome, he occasionally neglects to motivate his characters adequately and leaves a sour taste in the mouth of the auditor.

The fourth period (1609-1612) includes the three tragi-comedies, *Cymbeline, The Winter's Tale,* and *The Tempest.* With these plays Shakespeare begins a tradition, later carried almost to an absurdity by his young contemporaries Beaumont and Fletcher—the tragedy suddenly turned into a comedy. Although some critics call these plays decadent, *The Tempest* certainly does not deserve this epithet; it is a superb poetic achievement and one of Shakespeare's great plays.

## To the Reader.

This Figure, that thou here seest put,
 It was for gentle Shakespeare cut;
Wherein the Grauer had a strife
 with Nature, to out-doo the life:
O, could he but haue drawne his wit
 As well in brasse, as he hath hit
His face; the Print would then surpasse
 All, that was euer writ in brasse.
But, since he cannot, Reader, looke
 Not on his Picture, but his Booke.

B. I.

# COMEDIES

# OF

# WILLIAM SHAKESPEARE

# LOVE'S LABOUR'S LOST

## Cast of Characters

### *Main Characters*

FERDINAND, the King of Navarre, plans a quiet period of study, only to have it disrupted, rudely and quickly.

BIRON, a courtier of the King's, does not like the King's plan, but he finally joins the others until he meets Rosaline.

LONGAVILLE, another courtier, fails in his pledge because of Katharine.

DUMAIN, another courtier, cannot resist Maria.

THE PRINCESS OF FRANCE visits Navarre on a diplomatic mission and spoils the King's plan for austere living.

ROSALINE
MARIA } visit Navarre with the Princess and conquer Biron, Longaville, and Dumain.
KATHARINE

### *Supporting Characters*

DON ADRIANO DE ARMADO, a man of little wit but a great many words

BOYET, a lord accompanying the Princess of France

COSTARD, a clown, but wise enough to see through his betters

DULL, a well-named constable

A FORESTER

HOLOFERNES, another wordy fellow, a schoolmaster

MERCADE, a lord accompanying the Princess of France

MOTH, Armado's page

SIR NATHANIEL, a curate, who chatters windily but not too wisely

JAQUENETTA, a country wench

(Attendants, Lords)

(Place: *Navarre, at and near the King's palace*)

BACKGROUND. Probably first performed about 1588, this play was first printed in 1598. No known source has been discovered, though it may have been, in part, based on an incident related in Marguerite of Valois' *Memoires*. The play is noteworthy in that it contains a much greater proportion of rhymed lines than does any other Shakespearean play.

## ACT BY ACT ANALYSIS

**ACT I.** Ferdinand, King of Navarre, proposes to his courtiers, Biron, Longaville, and Dumain, that they go into a retreat together for three years, devoting themselves to scholarly pursuits. The King asks the courtiers to sign a pledge to live in absolute austerity. They shall see no women, shall fast one day a week, shall dine but once on other days, shall sleep but three hours a night. Biron, though he thinks the terms of withdrawal too harsh, finally signs with the others. The King also orders that all his subjects likewise abstain from any joys of the flesh. The only entertainment the courtiers will have will be the chatter of Costard, a clown, and Armado, a foolish Spanish gentleman. Costard is the first to be found guilty of consorting with a girl, Jaquenetta, and he is sentenced to a week's fasting in prison (i). Armado, who is ordered to be Costard's keeper, loves Jaquenetta too, and though fearful of the consequences, the foolish gentleman prepares to compose sonnets to her (ii).

**ACT II.** Ferdinand, some time before, had lent a sum of money to the King of France. Now the King's daughter arrives upon a diplomatic mission concerning the loan. The King listens to her suit, which cannot be settled until the next day when certain papers will have arrived. He prepares a tent for her and her retinue outside the gates, for (because of his vow) he cannot admit her. Ferdinand's courtiers immediately pair off with the Princess' ladies (i).

**ACT III.** Armado frees Costard in order that the clown may carry a letter to Jaquenetta. Biron meets the messenger and likewise entrusts him with a letter—this one to be delivered to Rosaline, one of the Princess' retinue (i).

**ACT IV.** Costard, of course, gets the letters mixed, and the one intended for Jaquenetta is delivered to the Princess (i).

Jaquenetta takes the letter she has received to Nathaniel (a curate) to have it read. The pedant, Holofernes, points out that this letter is really from Biron to Rosaline and directs Jaquenetta to carry it to the King (ii).

Biron conceals himself and spies upon the King as he reads a love poem. As Longaville enters, the King drops the paper and hides too. Longaville is composing a sonnet to Maria, one of the Princess' ladies. As Dumain enters, Longaville, too, hides. Dumain is also composing a poem—to Katharine, another of the Princess' retinue. Longaville now accosts Dumain, and is in turn accosted by the King, who accuses the courtiers of breaking their oath. But Biron now steps out of hiding and accuses the King of likewise being in love—with the Princess. Biron, however, is not long allowed to maintain his pretense of living up to the pledge. For Jaquenetta enters with Costard and brings the king Biron's letter to Rosaline. Now all the gentlemen realize that each alike has broken faith. Just as wholeheartedly as when they had sworn asceticism, they now swear to "woo these girls of France." They plan an entertainment for the ladies in order to help further their suits (iii).

**ACT V.**  The gentlemen approach the Princess and her court disguised as Russian masquers and woo the visitors, but the ladies have been forewarned by the spirited Boyet, have masked and exchanged favors so that their identities are confused. Returning in their own characters, the men are ridiculed by the ladies (ii). The minor characters have meanwhile prepared a "masque of the Nine Worthies" (i). When it is presented, it turns out a ridiculous failure. At the height of the merriment, a messenger brings word that the King of France is dead. Now the ladies must leave, and they inform the King and his courtiers that they will not listen to any serious proposals for a year. Further, the King must retire to a monastery for that year, and Biron must use his wit for the benefit of sufferers in hospitals. As the ladies prepare to leave, it is evident that, for the present at least, the labors of the lovers are lost (ii).

# COMEDY OF ERRORS

## Cast of Characters

### Main Characters

ANTIPHOLUS OF EPHESUS, an identical twin to Antipholus of Syracuse, has been lost from his family for many years but is finally restored.

ANTIPHOLUS OF SYRACUSE, has spent five years searching for his lost brother.

DROMIO OF EPHESUS, an identical twin to Dromio of Syracuse and a servant of Antipholus of Ephesus, is often beaten for the mistakes of his double.

DROMIO OF SYRACUSE, the counterpart of Dromio of Ephesus and the servant of Antipholus of Syracuse, likewise has difficulties because of mistaken identity.

ADRIANA, the jealous wife of Antipholus of Ephesus, cannot account for the strange actions of her supposed husband.

LUCIANA, the sister of Adriana, finds a husband where she thinks herself least likely to find one.

AEGEON, a merchant of Syracuse, finds a long-lost son.

AEMILIA, wife of Aegeon, becomes an abbess and renounces the world, but is finally returned to it with her husband and her reunited family.

### Supporting Characters

ANGELO, a goldsmith
BALTHAZAR, a merchant
COURTESAN
FIRST MERCHANT

LUCE, Adriana's servant
PINCH, a schoolmaster
SECOND MERCHANT
SOLINUS, Duke of Ephesus

(Attendants, jailer, officers)

(Place: *Ephesus*)

BACKGROUND. This play was probably (though not certainly) written about 1589 or 1590 and was first printed in 1623. Its chief source is the *Menaechmi* of Plautus, and the main plot follows that of the earlier play quite closely. Part of one scene (III, i) is taken from another play by Plautus, the *Amphitruo*. The reunion of the twins' parents is probably inspired by the story of Apollonius of Tyre, long an English favorite. Shakespeare's chief addition to the play consists in adding the further complication of twin servants.

## ACT BY ACT ANALYSIS

**ACT I.** Syracuse and Ephesus are enemy cities. Each has laws forbidding citizens of the other to enter, and those captured are subject to a fine of one thousand marks. Those unable to pay are put to death. Aegeon, a merchant of Syracuse, has been captured in Ephesus and is unable to pay his fine. He has been brought before Solinus, ruler of the city. The Duke sympathizes with the unfortunate merchant but tells him that even he, as ruler, is powerless to break the laws of the city in order to free him. In answer to the Duke's questions, Aegeon tells his reason for being in the city. He has two sons, he says, who are identical twins. The sons have a pair of servants who are also identical twins. Years ago one son, together with his mother and one of the servants, was separated from the rest of the family in a storm at sea. The remaining son, upon reaching young manhood, set out to find his lost brother. But after five years he had not returned. Aegeon, searching for the second son, has come to Ephesus and has, unfortunately, been captured (i).

Meanwhile, Antipholus of Syracuse (hereafter Antipholus S.), who has also just arrived in Ephesus, sends his servant, Dromio S., with a purse of money to the inn where they have been staying. Dromio of Ephesus (the identical twin of Dromio S.) enters and bids Antipholus S. to hurry lest he be late for dinner. (He thinks Antipholus S. is Antipholus E., the other twin and his master.) Antipholus S. asks about the money, but Dromio E., of course, proclaims complete ignorance concerning it. Antipholus S., angered, beats him and Dromio E. runs away (ii).

**ACT II.** Adriana, wife of Antipholus E., waits for her husband, who is late for dinner. Dromio E. tells her of his strange encounter with the man he believes to be his master. The waiting wife is immediately consumed with jealousy, imagining that another woman is detaining her husband. Her sister, Luciana, tries to soothe her (i).

Antipholus S. meets Dromio S. and scolds him for what he thinks was his servant's previous jesting. Dromio S. is, of course, completely ignorant of the whole episode. Antipholus S., again angered, beats him. Adriana enters and berates Antipholus S. His claim to be a stranger infuriates her all the more. Finally, half thinking himself insane, Antipholus S. is led off to dinner (ii).

**ACT III.** Before his house Antipholus E. arranges with a goldsmith to deliver a golden chain to his wife on the morrow. He berates Dromio E. for telling a wild tale about a purse of money and a beating he claims his master gave him. Antipholus E. has brought Balthazar, a merchant, home to dinner. Dromio S., however, will not admit them; nor will Adriana nor her servant, Luce. Antipholus E. wishes to force his way in, but Balthazar dissuades him on the grounds that such a row will ruin his wife's reputation. They depart for dinner elsewhere. Antipholus E. says that he will give the chain he is having made to another woman (i).

Luciana chides Antipholus S. for his conduct. Antipholus S. proclaims himself a total stranger to Adriana, but says that he loves her (Luciana). Dromio S. enters, chattering that a strange and horrible woman has claimed him as husband. Antipholus S. decides that the town must be bewitched and sends Dromio S. to see if any ships are leaving, so that they may leave the frightening place. His fears seem to be borne out when Angelo, the goldsmith, enters and insists upon his accepting the chain which the smith claims Antipholus has ordered (ii).

**ACT IV.** Antipholus E. sends Dromio E. to buy a rope's end with which to discipline his household; then he meets the goldsmith, who asks payment for the chain. Antipholus E. denies having received it. Angelo needs the money to pay a merchant who has a claim against him. When Antipholus E. refuses to pay, the merchant has Angelo arrested. Angelo, in turn, has Antipholus E. arrested. Dromio S. enters and tells Antipholus E. that he has secured passage on a boat which is ready to leave. Antipholus E. thinks him insane and sends him to Adriana for money to satisfy Angelo (i).

Adriana and Luciana discuss the strange behavior of the man they believe to be Adriana's husband. Dromio S. enters and asks for money to redeem the arrested Antipholus E. (ii). The servant secures the money and takes it to Antipholus S. who, of course, knows nothing about the situation. A courtesan asks Antipholus S. for the chain, which she claims he has promised her in return for a ring she has given him. Each is convinced of the other's madness, and Antipholus S. is more certain than ever that he is in a land bewitched (iii).

When Dromio E. eventually finds Antipholus E., he gives his master the rope's end instead of the money Antipholus E. expects. Antipholus E. beats him. Adriana and Luciana appear, and Antipholus E. berates them for locking him out of his house. This act, of course, they deny. He also accuses them of plotting his arrest. Adriana denies his accusation and says that she sent Dromio with money to free him. Dromio E. denies the claim. Adriana, thinking Antipholus E. mad, has him put under restraint by Doctor Pinch and his assistants, after offering to pay the goldsmith. Antipholus S. and Dromio S. enter, their rapiers drawn, after their doubles have been taken away by the doctor. Believing that the men have escaped from the doctor, the ladies flee. Antipholus S. is even more firmly convinced that the land is bewitched and tells Dromio S. that he plans to leave the city at once (iv).

ACT V. Antipholus S. and Dromio S. meet Angelo in a street before a priory. The goldsmith accosts them. He points out that even now Antipholus S. is wearing the chain that has caused so much trouble. Antipholus S. declares that he never has denied that he received the chain, and challenges the merchant, who has accompanied Angelo and who joins with him in his accusation. Adriana and Luciana come in and plead with the merchant, claiming that Antipholus S. is mad. (They still mistake him, of course, for Antipholus E.) The abbess of the priory comes out and blames the supposed madness upon Adriana's jealous carping. She refuses to allow Adriana to remove her supposed husband, and takes him into the abbey. The Duke enters with Aegeon, bound for the place of execution.

Now a messenger adds to the confusion by rushing in to announce the escape of the madman and his servant (i. e., Antipholus E. and Dromio E.). Soon they enter, and Aegeon believes the pair to be his son Antipholus S. and his servant, Dromio S. Antipholus E. accuses his wife of locking him out of his own house. Then he recounts all the evil things that have befallen him. Angelo repeats his story about the chain, and the confusion grows deeper; for he confirms Antipholus E.'s story that he was locked from his house. Aegeon now calls on Antipholus E., as his son, to pay his fine and save his life. Antipholus E., of course, does not recognize his father. Now the abbess comes in, with Antipholus S. and Dromio S.—at last the doubles are brought together. The threads are immediately unwound. The twins are sorted out, and the abbess is disclosed as Aemilia, Aegeon's wife and the mother of the twins (i).

# THE TWO GENTLEMEN OF VERONA

## Cast of Characters

### Main Characters

VALENTINE, a "gentleman of Verona," learns that friends are not always to be trusted in matters of love.

PROTEUS, the other "gentleman" of the title, proves himself a most unworthy friend and inconstant lover.

JULIA disguises herself as a page in order to be near her fickle lover, Proteus.

SILVIA, Valentine's beloved, will have no part of Proteus' blandishments or Thurio's "wailful" sonnets.

THURIO foolishly enlists the aid of false Proteus in his suit for the fair Silvia.

THE DUKE OF MILAN, Silvia's father, is unable to prevent his daughter's marrying whom she chooses.

### Supporting Characters

ANTONIO, father of Proteus

EGLAMOUR, Silvia's faithful friend

HOST, where Julia stays

LAUNCE, a clown and Proteus' servant

LUCETTA, Julia's waiting woman

OUTLAWS

SPEED, a clown and Valentine's servant

PANTHINO, servant to Antonio

(Musicians, Servants)

(Place: *Verona; Milan; and a forest between Milan and Mantua*)

BACKGROUND. Surmises concerning the date of the play's composition and performance vary from 1590 to 1592, but most modern critics agree in assigning it a date not later than 1592. It was not printed until the First Folio edition of 1623. The ultimate source is a Spanish pastoral, *Diana Enamorada,* written by Jorge de Montmayor. Shakespeare's immediate source is probably a lost play, *Felix and Philiomena,* acted at Greenwich in 1584.

## ACT BY ACT ANALYSIS

**ACT I.** As Valentine prepares to leave for the court of the Duke of Milan, he twits his friend Proteus (too much in love with Julia to think of leaving) for remaining behind. After Valentine leaves, his servant, Speed, enters; and Proteus questions him about a letter to Julia he has asked the loutish servant to deliver (i). Meanwhile Lucetta has shown the letter to Julia, who pretends no interest; but after tearing up the missive in a pretended rage, she tenderly gathers the scraps and deciphers the message (ii).

Now Proteus' pursuit of Julia is cut short by his father, who announces his plan to send Proteus (like Valentine) to the court of the Duke of Milan. Though Proteus pleads for an extension of time, he is ordered to leave the next day (iii).

**ACT II.** In Milan Valentine has also fallen in love. The object of this love, the fair Silvia, pretends indifference, but shows her interest in the young man by persuading him to write letters to a "friend"—a device the cunning Speed immediately recognizes as a means of wooing Valentine by having him send letters to himself (i). Proteus arrives in Milan (iv), after exchanging rings with Julia as a love remembrance (ii). Once in Milan, however, the flighty young lord immediately falls in love with Valentine's sweetheart, Silvia (vi). Valentine asks his friend to help him elope with the girl (iv), but Proteus, his head filled with amorous ideas of his own, treacherously plans to betray the elopement to the Duke (her father) and to win her for himself. The Duke, knowing nothing of the sly young man's intentions, plans for her to marry Thurio, a foolish gentleman (vi).

Now Julia, left behind in Verona, plans to follow Proteus to Milan, dressed as a page (vii).

**ACT III.** Proteus betrays his friend by telling the Duke of the coming elopement. The Duke, after promising not to tell Valentine who has betrayed him, meets the young lover and tricks him into showing the Duke his letter to Silvia and the rope ladder he plans to use for the elopement. The Duke banishes Valentine, and Proteus carries his treachery further by consoling the heartsick youth and offering to deliver any letters Valentine wishes to send to Silvia (i). Proteus now arranges with the Duke and Thurio to slander Valentine to Silvia. The Duke believes that he can be trusted in such an assignment since his love for Julia is so well known. As part of his plan of deceit, Proteus suggests that Thurio push his own cause by writing "wailful" sonnets to Silvia (ii).

**ACT IV.** In the forest, the banished Valentine is captured by outlaws. The youth tells them that he has been banished for slaying a man; and the outlaws, impressed, make him the captain of their band (i). Back in Milan, Proteus is having little success with his treacherous suit for Silvia's love. Julia has by now reached Milan. She hears Proteus singing (the famous "Who is Silvia?") and laments that Proteus no longer loves her. When Silvia tells Proteus that she despises him for his treachery, Julia listens, heartbroken (ii). In order to be near her faithless lover, Julia, still disguised as a page, enters his services, under the pseudonym, Sebastian. She performs the hateful task of carrying to Silvia her own ring (the love token she had given Proteus) together with a letter (iv). But Silvia has plans of her own. With the aid of Eglamour, a faithful friend, she decides to escape to Mantua, where she has heard that Valentine is living (iii).

**ACT V.** Silvia meets Eglamour at an abbey, and the couple flee (i). Her father, the Duke, hears of her flight almost immediately and organizes a posse to pursue her (ii). The outlaw band captures Silvia (iii), but Proteus rescues her. Since she is still cold to him, he threatens to force her to his desire. Valentine, who has overheard this threat, confronts Proteus, who immediately admits his error and begs forgiveness, which Valentine grants, after first generously offering to abandon his suit in favor of his friend. Julia, hearing Valentine's offer, faints; and the ring which Proteus has given her discloses her true identity. Proteus, repentant, reaffirms his love for Julia. The Duke enters with Thurio, prisoner of the outlaws. Valentine threatens Thurio, who hastily withdraws his suit for Silvia's hand. The Duke gives all his blessing, admonishes Thurio for his lack of aggressiveness, and pardons the outlaws (iv).

# A MIDSUMMER-NIGHT'S DREAM

## Cast of Characters

### *Main Characters*

THESEUS, Duke of Athens, has his wedding revels interrupted by strange and amusing antics.

LYSANDER, an Athenian youth, loves Hermia until Robin bewitches him for a time.

DEMETRIUS, an Athenian youth, loves Hermia too, but the fairies soon change this one-sided affection.

HERMIA loves Lysander, though for a time he does not return this love.

HELENA, loves Demetrius but, after being loved by no one, is for a time loved by too many.

HIPPOLYTA, Queen of the Amazons, is betrothed to Theseus.

OBERON, the Fairy King, gets the changeling boy he wants.

TITANIA, Queen of the Fairies, makes love to an ass before her eyes are opened.

ROBIN GOODFELLOW, a Puck, is the elfin jester of King Oberon's fairy court.

BOTTOM, a weaver, wears an ass's head with great nonchalance and with even a greater nonchalance plays Pyramus in the revels.

### *Supporting Characters*

| | |
|---|---|
| COBWEB, a fairy | PEASEBLOSSOM, a fairy |
| EGEUS, Hermia's father | PHILOSTRATE, master of the revels |
| FLUTE, a bellows mender | QUINCE, a carpenter |
| MOTH, a fairy | SNOUT, a tinker |
| MUSTARDSEED, a fairy | SNUG, a joiner |
| | STARVELING, a tailor |

(Other fairies in Oberon's and Titania's retinues, Attendants)

(Place: *Athens and a wood nearby*)

BACKGROUND. This play was first printed in 1600. The date of its first performance has not been established exactly, but it was probably 1594 or 1595. The plot is original but has several sources from which 'details are drawn. These include Chaucer's *Knight's Tale,* and his *Legend of Good Women;* Plutarch's *Life of Theseus;* Montemayor's *Diana;* Ovid's *Metamorphoses.*

## ACT BY ACT ANALYSIS

**ACT I.** Theseus, Duke of Athens, about to marry Hippolyta, the Queen of the Amazons, plans extensive revels to celebrate the occasion. He is soon disturbed, however, by a domestic squabble. Hermia, a fair Athenian girl, loves Lysander; but her father has promised her to a rival, Demetrius. The father, Egeus, now complains to Theseus of his daughter's willfulness. The Duke upholds Egeus; Hermia, he says, must either marry according to her father's wishes or accept one of two unpleasant alternatives: she must either die or "abjure forever the society of men."

In order to escape this judgment, Lysander and Hermia plan to elope, and arrange to meet in a wood nearby. Unwisely, as it turns out, they confide their plans to Helena, who is madly in love with Demetrius. She immediately plans to tell Demetrius, hoping to ingratiate herself with him (**i**).

Meanwhile, a group of artisans meet to discuss their plans to play an "interlude" as one of the revels for the Duke. The actors arrange to meet the following night for rehearsal—their meeting place to be the same wood chosen by the lovers (**ii**).

**ACT II.** In this very wood a quarrel is raging between the rulers of the fairies about the custody of a "changeling," a little Indian boy. Titania, the Queen, has the boy and flatly refuses to give him up to her husband, Oberon, King of the Fairies. Angry with his queen, Oberon sends his fairy jester, Robin Goodfellow, to find a flower whose juice has magical properties. Rubbed upon her eyelids while she sleeps, this juice will make the queen love madly the first living thing she sees upon awakening, "Be it lion, bear, or wolf, or bull." While waiting for Robin's return, Oberon overhears Demetrius and Helena talking. Helena has betrayed the eloping couple to Demetrius, who has gone in search of them. Oberon, overhearing him scold Helena, plans to make matters right between the quarreling mortals. He sends Robin to rub some of the magic juice upon Demetrius' eyes after the youth has gone to sleep (i), then goes to find Titania, who sleeps in the wood near where Hermia and Lysander are also sleeping. Oberon anoints her eyes, while Robin finds the sleeping Lysander and squeezes the magic juice upon him, mistaking him for Demetrius. Demetrius, followed by the persistent Helena, wanders by, and Helena awakens Lysander. Since Helena is the first living thing he sees upon awakening, Lysander immediately loves her. Leaving Hermia, he follows Helena into the woods (ii).

**ACT III.** Robin overhears the clowns rehearsing their "interlude." The knavish elf enchants Bottom, changing his head into a donkey's. Titania awakes from her sleep nearby, sees Bottom, and is hopelessly smitten, ass's head and all (i). Meanwhile Hermia has wandered off in search of Lysander. She finds Demetrius instead and accuses him of murdering her lover. Robin and Oberon witness this byplay and realize that the sprite has mistakenly anointed the eyes of the wrong "Athenian youth." After Hermia leaves, Demetrius goes to sleep and the fairies anoint his eyes, while Oberon sends Robin to bring Helena so that she will be the first person seen by the sleeping youth when he awakens. This stratagem works admirably, but now both Lysander and Demetrius love Helena, and they begin to quarrel over her, both now spurning Hermia. When the two youths leave to find a place to fight, Oberon orders Robin to lead them astray by false voices until they are so tired that they will fall asleep. The elf is then to apply an antidote to Lysander's eyes so that he will love Hermia again (ii).

**ACT IV.** Oberon, who has obtained the changeling from the betwitched Queen, sees her sleeping with the foolish Bottom clasped in her arms. Pitying her, he applies the antidote to her eyes and removes the enchantment from Bottom's head. The four lovers, sleeping nearby, are discovered by Theseus, Hippolyta, Egeus, and a retinue, who have come to hunt in the woods. The angry father demands that Theseus invoke the law against Hermia. But when Demetrius tells Egeus that he no longer loves Hermia, Theseus approves the new pairing off of the lovers (i).

**ACT V.** The three couples—Theseus and Hippolyta, Lysander and Hermia, Demetrius and Helena—happily gather in Theseus' palace to watch the wedding revels. The clowns present their ridiculous play, "the most lamentable comedy, and most cruel death of Pyramus and Thisbe." When the mortals have gone, the fairies dance and sing. Finally Robin Goodfellow is left to close with an epilogue asking the audience's approval (i).

# THE MERCHANT OF VENICE

## Cast of Characters

### Main Characters

ANTONIO, the merchant of Venice, is willing to risk his life to help his friend's courtship.

BASSANIO borrows Antonio's money with nearly fatal consequences for his friend, but chooses the right box and wins a bride.

PORTIA, Bassanio's bride, shows that women can be shrewd as well as beautiful. She makes a skillful and convincing lawyer.

GRATIANO accompanies his friend, Bassanio, to Belmont where he, too, finds a wife.

NERISSA, Portia's waiting woman, chooses Gratiano for a husband.

LORENZO, Antonio's friend, wins Shylock's daughter for a bride.

JESSICA, Shylock's daughter, deserts her father, taking a goodly share of his treasure with her.

SHYLOCK, the money lender, is so bent on a bloodthirsty revenge that he is caught in his own trap.

LAUNCELOT GOBBO leaves Shylock's service for Bassanio's.

### Supporting Characters

BALTHAZAR, Portia's servant

THE DUKE OF VENICE, who cannot abrogate his own laws

LEONARDO, Bassanio's servant

OLD GOBBO, Launcelot's father

THE PRINCE OF ARRAGON

The PRINCE OF MOROCCO

SALANIO. ⎫
SALARINO. ⎬ Antonio's friends
SALERIO. ⎭

STEPHANO, Portia's servant
TUBAL, Shylock's friend
(Attendants, Nobles of Venice, Officers of the Court, Servants)
(Place: *Venice and Belmont*)

BACKGROUND. This play was first printed in 1600 but was probably acted between 1594 and 1597. The plot, for the most part, comes from a story collection, *Il Pecorone,* written by Giovanni Fiorentino in 1378. Portia's plan for selecting her suitor can be traced to a story in the *Gesta Romanorum,* a medieval collection of tales translated in 1577. Minor details such as Jessica's part were probably suggested by similar situations in Marlowe's *Jew of Malta;* and a lost play, *The Jew,* mentioned by Stephen Gosson in his *School of Abuse* in 1579 may well have already incorporated the various story elements into a form roughly approximating that of the play as we know it.

## ACT BY ACT ANALYSIS

**ACT I.** Antonio, though his own money is tied up in shipping ventures, promises to help his friend Bassanio raise a large sum to be used in wooing the fair Portia (**i**). Portia's dead father has extracted a promise from the girl that she select her husband by means of a lottery in which prospective suitors must choose correctly from three boxes—one of gold, one of silver, and one of lead. None of the suitors besieging her pleases Portia except Bassanio (**ii**), who with Antonio's help has now arranged to borrow three thousand ducats from Shylock, the money lender. Despite Bassanio's protest, Antonio agrees to forfeit a pound of flesh if the loan plus interest is not repaid in time. This condition the wily Shylock pretends is merely part of a merry jest, though he really hates Antonio for several reasons: Antonio is a Christian; Antonio lends money without interest; and Antonio has reviled Shylock as a usurer (**iii**).

**ACT II.** Launcelot Gobbo leaves Shylock's service for that of Bassanio (**ii**). When he tells Shylock's daughter, Jessica, that he is leaving, she gives him a letter to deliver to Lorenzo, his new master's guest (**iii**). Lorenzo receives the letter and tells his friends that Jessica is planning to elope with him. He plans a masque and street parade which will pass her house and give her an opportunity to slip away (**iv**). When Shylock leaves home that evening to attend a banquet with the "prodigal

Christian," he cautions Jessica to guard his treasures well and warns her not to watch the masquers who, Launcelot has told her, will pass by (v). Jessica, however, joins the paraders, disguised as a boy, and succeeds in eloping with Lorenzo (vi). Since Shylock suspects Antonio of complicity in the elopement, Antonio's friends are worried about the money lender's reprisal when they hear rumors that Antonio's ships are being lost in storms (viii).

Meanwhile, in Belmont, the Prince of Morocco (vii) and the Prince of Arragon (ix) try their luck at choosing the right box and Portia for a bride—both fail.

**ACT III.** Now Bassanio enters the lottery; he chooses the right box, and Portia pledges her troth with a ring. Gratiano announces his love for Nerissa, Portia's waiting woman, and she accepts him (ii). Back in Venice Shylock laments his daughter's desertion, swearing to avenge himself upon Antonio if the chance presents itself. He listens carefully when his countryman, Tubal, brings news of mounting disasters among Antonio's ships (i). As the disaster multiplies, Salerio is sent to Belmont with a letter for Bassanio—a letter that tells of Antonio's total bankruptcy. Though Portia offers to pay twenty times the forfeit, her friends tell her that Shylock has already refused payment; avid for revenge upon the hated Christian, he insists upon his pound of flesh. In order to help her new husband's friend, Portia sends Bassanio with money to attempt, at least, to save Antonio (ii). After Bassanio leaves, Portia entrusts her estate to Lorenzo. She and Nerissa, she says, plan to "live in prayer and contemplation" at a nunnery until Bassanio returns. The wily girl then sends a letter to her cousin, Dr. Bellario, a learned jurist; and she and Nerissa follow their husbands to Venice, disguised as men (iv). While Lorenzo and Jessica pass the time in felicitous repose in Belmont (v), Shylock prepares to spring his trap upon the unfortunate Antonio. He taunts Antonio in the street; even the Duke, he says, cannot save Antonio now, since to abate the law would impeach the reputation of Venice for justice (iii).

**ACT IV.** In court, the Duke requests mercy for Antonio, but Shylock is adamant: mercy does not interest him, he insists upon justice. Now Portia enters the case, disguised as Balthazar, a learned young judge, bearing a letter of recommendation from her cousin, Dr. Bellario. She also asks Shylock for mercy and offers him three times his amount due—still he refuses. Now Portia springs her trap. Shylock may have his pound of flesh she says, but if he takes one drop of blood, he shall lose all his lands in forfeit. Shylock, realizing that he is trapped, is now willing to accept money instead of flesh; but Portia insists that he shall have only the penalty if he refuses the payment. Furthermore, she warns, if he takes the smallest fraction too much or too little, he shall die and all his goods shall be forfeit to the state. Refused even his principal, Shylock attempts to slink from the court, but now Portia tells him of another law; it is decreed, she says, that if any alien attempts to take the life of a Venetian, one-half of his goods shall go to him upon whom the attempt was made, the other half to the State, and his life shall be at the mercy of the Duke. The Duke spares his life but takes his half of the estate. Antonio says that he will be content with one-half of his share provided that Shylock bequeath his remaining estate to Lorenzo at his death, but before he will grant this concession, he says, Shylock must become a Christian. Pressed to take payment for her skillful defense of Antonio, Portia asks for the ring she has formerly given Bassanio. Though he protests, Bassanio finally parts with the love token (i). Nerissa, also still disguised, tells Portia that she will see if she can persuade Gratiano to part with the ring she has formerly given him (ii).

ACT V. Portia and Nerissa return to Belmont, pretending that they are merely coming back from the nunnery. Nerissa upbraids Gratiano for not having the ring she gave him. Now Portia pretends to find that Bassanio's ring, too, is gone. She scolds him first; then she and Nerissa produce the rings. After they tease their husbands by telling them that they have slept with the doctor and his clerk in return for the tokens, they finally reveal that Portia was the learned Doctor Balthazar and Nerissa his clerk (i).

# THE TAMING OF THE SHREW

## Cast of Characters

### Main Characters

PETRUCHIO, a madcap fellow, is more than a match for the bad-tempered Katharina.

KATHARINA, the bad-tempered sister, is not only tamed herself but lectures other erring brides.

LUCENTIO poses as schoolmaster to win Bianca.

BIANCA, the younger sister, is as amiable as the elder is shrewish.

HORTENSIO also woos Bianca but cannot stomach a schoolmaster as rival.

TRANIO, Lucentio's servant, doubles admirably for his master.

BAPTISTA insists that his daughter Katharina marry before Bianca.

### Supporting Characters

CURTIS, Petruchio's servant

GREMIO, another suitor of Bianca

GRUMIO, Petruchio's servant

BIONDELLO, Lucentio's servant

A LORD

A PEDANT

CHRISTOPHER SLY, a tinker

VINCENTIO, Lucentio's father

WIDOW, Hortensio's bride

(Hostess, Page, Players, Huntsmen, Tailor, Haberdasher, Servants)

(Place: *Padua and Petruchio's house in the country*)

BACKGROUND. The first printed form of this play is that of the First Folio (1623). It was probably presented about 1594, though dates as early as 1592 and as late as 1602 have been suggested.

A similar play, *The Taming of A Shrew,* of unknown authorship, presented in 1594, is probably the immediate source for the play, though some scholars believe that the earlier play was also written by Shakespeare and that *A Shrew* is merely an early version of *The Shrew*.

## ACT BY ACT ANALYSIS

INTRODUCTION: (A Prologue.) Christopher Sly, a vagabond tinker, lies dead drunk before an alehouse. A passing lord, seeing him there, decides a joke upon the wretch will make good sport. He orders his followers to scoop the fellow up, place him in the best bed in the lord's best room, cover him with jewels and surround him with servants. Bartholomew, his page, is to dress as a woman and play "wife" to the tinker (i). When Sly awakens, his "servants" persuade him that he has slept for fifteen years. Now players whom the lord has engaged enter and present to Sly *The Taming of the Shrew* (ii).

ACT I. Baptista, a rich Padua merchant, has two daughters. The elder daughter, Katharina, has a violently disagreeable disposition; and no suitors have appeared for her hand. But Baptista insists that the beautiful and amiable younger daughter, Bianca, shall not marry until her elder sister has married. Lucentio, a newcomer to Padua, falls in love with Bianca at first sight and plans to gain access to her by posing as a schoolteacher, while his servant Tranio shall impersonate his master (i). Hortensio, another suitor, plans to gain access to Bianca by posing as a musician. Now Petruchio enters Padua in search of a rich wife, and Hortensio and Gremio (suitors for Bianca) arrange for him to meet the shrewish sister, whom he believes he can tame.

ACT II. Petruchio calls upon his prospective father-in-law. He brings Hortensio with him, disguised as a musician. The two are accompanied by the other suitor, Gremio, who believes that Lucentio is presenting Gremio's case to Bianca. Hortensio's musical endeavors are cut short by Kate, who hangs his lute about his ears. Petruchio attempts to take Katharine by storm; and, after they battle merrily, he tells Baptista that they will marry on the following Sunday. The way is now cleared for

Bianca to marry. Baptista, to settle things among the quarreling lovers, tells them that the one who offers the greatest dowry shall marry Bianca. Tranio (disguised as Lucentio) makes the largest offer, and Baptista agrees to accept his offer providing Lucentio's father will give assurance for it. Now Tranio tries to think of someone to impersonate Lucentio's father (i).

**ACT III.** Lucentio, disguised as a schoolteacher, introduces himself to Bianca. Hortensio does likewise while pretending to give a music lesson. Hortensio, who supposes Lucentio to be a simple pedant, is worried that the teacher may become a serious rival (i). Meanwhile Katharina makes ready for the wedding. Petruchio, however, fails to appear and Katharina weeps bitter tears of shame and rage. When the tardy groom finally makes his appearance, both he and his servant are wearing fantastic clothing. Petruchio's garb shocks the whole assemblage, but he insists on keeping it on for the wedding. He acts wildly through-out the wedding, and after the ceremonies he announces that he is leaving before the wedding feast, a thing unthinkable. Katharina objects with something of her old spirit, but Petruchio forces her to go with him (ii).

**ACT IV.** Petruchio brings Kate to his home, where he abuses his servants, and keeps her from eating by pretending that the meat is burned. Then the wild bridegroom takes Kate to her room and keeps her awake with his abuse. These strange actions are part of a plan to tame her (i). As a further step he humiliates her by pretending to disapprove of her new wardrobe and by forcing her to journey back to her father's house in old clothes (iii). On the way they meet Vincentio, journeying to Padua to see his son, Lucentio (v).

Back in Padua Hortensio sees that Bianca loves the disguised pedant and leaves his own disguise, scornfully condemning Bianca for leaving "a gentleman" and making "a god" of "such a cullion." Hortensio firmly vows not to court her any more but instead to marry a wealthy widow. The wily Tranio now carries out his plan to find a pseudo-father to guarantee Lucentio's dowry. He tricks an old man into pretending that he is Vincentio, the father, by telling him he will be put to death if he does not comply (ii). Baptista accepts the false Vincentio and they agree to meet to arrange a dowry. But Lucentio's servants advise their master to keep on his disguise a little while longer. They further advise him to slip away with Bianca and marry her secretly while the others think that he is escorting her to dinner (**iv**).

**ACT V.** Petruchio and the real Vincentio arrive at Lucentio's house in Padua, where Vincentio is refused admittance by the pseudo-Vincentio. Now Lucentio appears in his own guise, safely wedded to Bianca, and asks pardon of his father and new father-in-law. He confesses the whole trick (**i**). Everything being settled amicably, all parties gather to banquet at Lucentio's house. After being twitted for marrying a shrew, Petruchio wagers that his wife is the most obedient of all the new brides. Both Lucentio and Hortensio send for their wives, but both refuse to come. Katharina not only comes at once when Petruchio sends for her, a most thoroughly tamed shrew, but she also upbraids the other brides for not obeying their husbands and recites a moral lecture on the proper behavior of wives (**ii**).

# THE MERRY WIVES OF WINDSOR

## Cast of Characters

### *Main Characters*

SIR JOHN FALSTAFF, a fat and thoroughly roguish knight, gets his just deserts when he attempts to woo the merry wives of Windsor.

MRS. PAGE }
MRS. FORD } the merry wives, teach a jealous husband and a fat rogue a lesson, though Mrs. Page cannot secure the suitor of her choice for her daughter.

MR. FORD learns that jealousy is a bad business.

MR. PAGE trusts his wife completely, but gets an unexpected son-in-law.

MRS. QUICKLY plays both ends against the middle and promises to help all the parties concerned in their complicated love matches.

ANNE PAGE by trickery gets the lover of her choice.

FENTON, Anne Page's beloved

SHALLOW, a country justice, fails to help Slender's cause.

ABRAHAM SLENDER, Page's choice for his daughter's hand and Shallow's cousin

DOCTOR CAIUS is backed by Mrs. Page in his suit for Anne.

SIR HUGH EVANS makes an abortive attempt to fight a duel with Dr. Caius.

HOST of the Garter Inn, a genial, roguish fellow

PISTOL }
NYM } followers of Falstaff and even greater rogues than
BARDOLPH } their master

### *Supporting Characters*

WILLIAM PAGE, Page's son

ROBIN, Falstaff's page boy

JOHN RUGBY, Dr. Caius' servant

PETER SIMPLE, Slender's servant

(Servants to Page and Ford)

(Place: *Windsor and the surrounding neighborhood*)

BACKGROUND. This play appeared in two quarto editions (both much garbled) before the First Folio edition of 1623. There is a tradition dating from the eighteenth century that the play was written at the express command of Queen Elizabeth. It is usually believed, too, that *The Merry Wives* is a reworked version of an earlier play. The most likely ultimate source of the play is *The Tale of the Two Lovers of Pisa* in *Tarleton's Newes out of Purgatorie* (1590).

## ACT BY ACT ANALYSIS

**ACT I.** Justice Shallow and Sir Hugh Evans wish to arrange a marriage between Mistress Anne Page (who has a good dowry) and Abraham Slender, Shallow's cousin (**i**). Evans sends a letter to Mistress Quickly, asking her to intercede with Miss Page on Slender's behalf (**ii**). Meanwhile, at the Garter Inn, the roguish Sir John Falstaff is also making amorous plans. He will, he says, make love to both Mrs. Ford (who he has heard rules her husband's house) and to Mrs. Page, who also "bears the purse" of her family. He sends letters to the two women, but after he leaves the inn his two followers, Nym and Pistol, plan to betray their master to the husbands of the two women (**iii**). Mrs. Quickly receives Evans' letter and promises to help Slender all she can, though it turns out a little later that she has already promised another suitor, Fenton, the same thing. But the bearer of the letter is discovered by Dr. Caius, Mrs. Quickly's master, who also loves Anne Page. The irate doctor sends a message to Evans, the author of the letter, challenging him to a duel (**iv**).

**ACT II.** Mrs. Ford and Mrs. Page receive love letters from Falstaff and plan to hatch a plot against this "greasy knight"; but meanwhile Page and Ford are warned by Pistol and Nym that Falstaff plans to woo their wives. Ford, a very jealous man, arranges to be introduced to Falstaff as "Brook," (**i**) and when he meets the knight he offers to pay Falstaff to make love to Mrs. Ford; not trusting his wife, he wishes to test her. When

Falstaff agrees and Ford finds he already has an appointment with her, the jealous husband is furious. He immediately plans to surprise Falstaff with his wife. Just before this, Mrs. Quickly has come to Falstaff from Mrs. Ford and Mrs. Page with a message that Ford will be away from home between ten and eleven so that Falstaff can meet her at that time. Mrs. Page, she says, wants Falstaff to send his servant Robin as a go-between to arrange a meeting (ii). Dr. Caius has been waiting in a field to meet Sir Hugh Evans. The host of the Garter, sensing fine sport, offers to lead Caius to Anne Page's house (iii).

**ACT III.** The host, however, leads him to another field, where Sir Hugh Evans is waiting. The duel dissolves when the host confesses that he has purposely directed the antagonists to wait in different places, and the two make peace, vowing revenge upon the roguish host for his trick (i). Returning from the "dueling" field, the party meets the jealous Ford, who is on his way to (he thinks) surprise his wife with the villainous Falstaff (ii). Mrs. Page and Mrs. Ford have, in the meantime, planned a warm reception for the "greasy knight." While Falstaff is making impassioned speeches to Mrs. Ford, Mrs. Page rushes in to warn the couple that Ford is approaching with officers. Falstaff is hidden in a basket of dirty laundry, and servants carry the basket away to dump it (as had been previously arranged by the two women) in a foul ditch along the Thames (iii). At Page's house, Fenton (whom Anne really loves), is rebuffed by Anne's father, who prefers Slender as a suitor. But Mrs. Page's apparent friendliness toward Fenton promises another complication (iv). Falstaff, drying out at the Garter Inn, receives Mrs. Quickly, who apologizes for his plight and arranges another rendezvous with Mrs. Ford. Falstaff, unsuspecting, passes this information along to "Mr. Brook," the real Mr. Ford. Ford, now in a paroxysm of jealous rage, swears that he will catch the guilty pair this time (v).

**ACT IV.** After Mrs. Page learns that Falstaff has gone to Mrs. Ford's (i), she again comes to warn her friend of the jealous husband's approach. This time the merry wives dress the errant knight as Mrs. Ford's maid's aunt in order to slip him out of the house. Ford comes again, together with his friends, and this time searches the laundry basket but, of course, finds nothing. Spying the knight dressed as the fat old woman, whom he hates, Ford beats him soundly and drives him away (ii). Now the wives tell their husbands of the plot, and the whole group decides to catch the fat knight once more. Falstaff will be asked to meet the merry wives in a wood, disguised as a wood nymph, with horns on his head. Anne Page, as the queen of the fairies, accompanied by a group of children disguised as sprites, will surround Falstaff and pinch him black and blue. Then, when he has told the truth about the whole affair, he will be "mocked home to Windsor" (iv). So Mrs. Quickly bears Falstaff yet another letter (v). Now it transpires that more will happen in the wood than Mrs. Ford or Mrs. Page had planned. Fenton bears a tale to the host of the Garter. Page, he says, has instructed his daughter to slip away with Slender during the excitement and to marry him immediately. Mrs. Page has instructed Anne to slip away with Dr. Caius and to marry him. Both parents have arranged for the girl to wear distinctive dress so that the suitors will recognize her. But she and Fenton have arranged to slip off together, fooling both parents, and the host arranges to furnish a minister to marry them (vi).

**ACT V.** Falstaff, the insatiable, arranges with Mrs. Quickly for the last meeting (i). In the wood, Slender and Page arrange for Slender's abduction of Anne (ii), while Mrs. Page and Dr. Caius are also completing their plans (iii), and Sir Hugh Evans is giving some last minute coaching to the "fairies" (iv). Falstaff arrives and meets the merry wives; then the fairies descend upon him. While the "fairies" are tormenting the luckless knight, Slender and Caius each slip off with a boy they believe to be Anne Page. She, however, runs away with Fenton. The merry wives and their husbands approach Falstaff—a dejected rogue now—and reveal their true identity. Slender and Caius both return and tell how they were deceived. When Anne and Fenton come back, married, they find Page a forgiving father; and at Mrs. Page's suggestion, the party troops away to "laugh this sport o'er by a country fire" (v).

# MUCH ADO ABOUT NOTHING

## Cast of Characters

### *Main Characters*

CLAUDIO, a young lord of Florence, too easily believes ill of his sweetheart and almost loses her.

HERO, Claudio's sweetheart, pretends death to chasten her lover.

BENEDICK, a young lord of Padua, engages in a good deal of raillery with Beatrice before he succumbs to her.

BEATRICE finally accepts Benedick, but she will not quite admit publicly that she loves him.

DON PEDRO proves a worthy friend of Claudio, though he, too, believes that Hero has played Claudio false.

DON JOHN, Pedro's illegitimate brother, an evil, envious man, almost wrecks the lives of Claudio and Hero.

LEONATO, Hero's father and Beatrice's uncle, refuses to believe evil of his daughter.

### *Supporting Characters*

ANTONIO, Leonato's brother

BALTHASAR, follower of Don Pedro

BORACHIO, follower of Don John

A BOY

CONRADE, follower of Don John

DOGBERRY, a constable

FRIAR FRANCIS

MARGARET, Hero's waiting woman

A SEXTON

URSULA, Hero's waiting woman
VERGES, a headborough

(Messengers, Watchmen, Attendants)

(Place: *Messina*)

BACKGROUND. *Much Ado About Nothing* was first published as a quarto in 1600, after being performed during the winter of 1598-1599. Its chief source is the twenty-second tale in a collection of Italian *Novella* by Matteo Bandello, while the subplot is original with Shakespeare.

## ACT BY ACT ANALYSIS

**ACT I.** Benedick and Claudio come to Messina from the wars. Claudio promptly falls in love with Hero, while Benedick takes up an old game of bickering with Beatrice. Don Pedro, the military superior of the young men, promises to intercede with Leonato, Hero's father, on behalf of Claudio—in fact to make Claudio's proposal to Hero for him (**i**). Leonato is informed of the young man's intentions and is well pleased (**ii**). But when Don Pedro's bastard brother, John, hears of Claudio's intentions he rails against the young man and plans to block his marriage plans if possible (**iii**).

**ACT II.** John, helped by his man Borachio, immediately tries to thwart Claudio's plans. While, during a masquerade, Don Pedro is approaching Hero on Claudio's behalf, John comes to Claudio, who he pretends to think is Benedick. He tells Claudio that Don Pedro is really wooing Hero for himself and asks the pretended Benedick to dissuade Pedro from such a course, saying that Hero is unworthy. Pedro, though, summons Claudio and tells him that he has won Hero for the hopeful lover; and, elated by his success as a matchmaker, Pedro says that he will now make a match for Beatrice and Benedick (**i**). John now tries another plan. Borachio plans to persuade one of Hero's waiting ladies to impersonate Hero, then be discovered in a compromising situation with him (**ii**). Meanwhile Leonato and Claudio are helping Pedro arrange a match between Benedick and Beatrice. They, knowing Benedick is listening, chat for his benefit—Beatrice, they say, loves him. Benedick immediately begins to suspect double meanings in Beatrice's barbed remarks (**iii**).

**ACT III.** Hero and Ursula play the same game with Beatrice, who is completely taken in and immediately resolves to tame her own contemptuous spirit (**i**). John, intent upon his evil work, now tells Claudio that Hero is unfaithful, and the young man swears that if she is untrue he will shame her before the congregation on their wedding day (**ii**). But while Borachio and Conrade, his accomplice, are discussing Borachio's evil deed, they are overheard and captured by two watchmen, Dogberry and Verges (**iii**). The next day Hero prepares for the wedding ceremony, helped by her ladies in waiting (**iv**), while the watchmen tell Leonato of taking Borachio and Conrade. They wish Leonato to examine the culprits; but he, busy with the coming wedding, puts them off and tells them to examine the fellows themselves (**v**).

**ACT IV.** Claudio, true to his promise, (thinking Hero guilty) denounces her and shames her before the congregation. The poor girl swoons, and when Claudio and Pedro leave, they think her dead. The friar who was to perform the ceremony suggests that Leonato continue to pretend that Hero is dead while they investigate the case. Her supposed death, too, will soften Claudio's heart, and turn public censure to pity. Benedick now admits his love for Beatrice and she for him. She asks him, as a favor, to kill Claudio. At first he refuses and, as usual, she berates him (**i**). Dogberry and Verges examine Borachio and Conrade, who confess and implicate John. John, they say, has already fled. The sexton orders the knaves bound and brought before Leonato (**ii**).

**ACT V.** Now Claudio's friends turn against him. Leonato, Antonio, and Benedick all challenge Claudio to duel, accusing him of murdering the innocent Hero. When Dogberry and Verges bring in the rogues, Leonato tells Claudio that he must broadcast Hero's innocence to the people, then marry Leonato's niece whom he has never seen (**i**). Meanwhile, Beatrice is writing verses to Benedick. When he comes to her and tells her that he has challenged Claudio, she tells Benedick that she loves him (**ii**). Claudio places an epitaph on Hero's tomb, telling of her innocence and tragic death (**iii**) and comes to marry Leonato's niece as he has promised. Hero, masked, enters with her maid in waiting. Claudio, thinking that she is Leonato's niece, swears to marry her. At a tense moment, she unmasks and reveals herself as Hero. Beatrice now publicly accepts Benedick, not so much, she says jokingly, that she loves him, but to save his life, for she has heard that he was "in a consumption." A messenger enters and announces the capture of the evil John (**iv**).

# AS YOU LIKE IT

## Cast of Characters

### *Main Characters*

ORLANDO DE BOYS loses his patrimony for a while but regains it at last, together with his true love, Rosalind.

ROSALIND, the banished Duke's daughter, disguises herself as a boy called Ganymede, with whom her real lover practices courtship.

OLIVER DE BOYS tries to murder his brother Orlando, but conscience is awakened when Orlando saves his life. He falls in love with the disguised Celia.

CELIA, Duke Frederick's daughter, disguised as "Ganymede's" (Rosalind's) sister, Aliena, escapes to the forest with Rosalind. She is wooed and won by Oliver.

SILVIUS, a shepherd, loves Phebe but for a time is not loved in return.

PHEBE, beloved by Silvius, thinks herself in love with the masquerading "Ganymede" (Rosalind).

TOUCHSTONE, a clown, mocks and satirizes courtly life.

AUDREY, a country lass, is captured by Touchstone.

DUKE, banished to the forest of Arden by his brother, Frederick

DUKE FREDERICK finally restores his banished brother to power and leaves the world for a cloister.

JAQUES, a melancholy, philosophizing courtier

### *Supporting Characters*

ADAM, Oliver's servant

AMIENS, banished Duke's courtier

CHARLES, Frederick's wrestler

CORIN, a shepherd

DENNIS, Oliver's servant

JAQUES DE BOYS, brother of Orlando and Oliver
LE BEAU, courtier of the banished Duke
SIR OLIVER MARTEXT, a vicar
WILLIAM, a country fellow

(Hymen, Lords, Pages, Attendants)

(Place: *Oliver's house, the Duke Frederick's palace, Arden Forest*)

BACKGROUND. No printed edition of the play appears before that of the First Folio (1623). It was first performed in 1599 or 1600. The play is a dramatization of a pastoral tale called *Rosalynde, Euphues' Golden Legacie,* written by Thomas Lodge in 1590. This tale, in turn, is based on an early English poem *The Tale of Gamelyn,* which has at times (though not at present) been attributed to Chaucer.

## ACT BY ACT ANALYSIS

**ACT I.** Orlando, the younger son of Sir Rowland de Boys, rebels at being kept a virtual prisoner by his elder brother, Oliver. He plans to leave, but Oliver, who hates him and wishes to keep his patrimony, arranges with Charles, wrestler for the Duke Frederick, to kill or cripple the youth (**i**). Orlando, however, manages to throw and injure the redoubtable fellow, and his victory is witnessed by Rosalind, daughter of the banished Duke, and her cousin Celia, daughter of the present duke, Frederick. Rosalind instantly falls in love with the young man and he with her (**ii**), but as soon as Orlando has left, Duke Frederick orders Rosalind banished. She plans to flee to her father in the forest, accompanied by Celia (**iii**).

**ACT II.** When Duke Frederick finds his daughter gone, he orders Oliver brought before him if Orlando cannot be found, since he has heard that Orlando has accompanied the girls (**ii**). Meanwhile Orlando has returned home and discovers that Oliver plans to murder him. He flees to Arden Forest, together with old Adam, a faithful servant (**iii**). Rosalind and Celia also escape to Arden Forest, Rosalind disguised as a youth, "Ganymede," and Celia as the youth's sister, "Aliena." They meet two shepherds, Corin and Silvius, and arrange to buy a shepherd's hut, a flock, and pasture (**iv**). In another part of the forest the banished Duke discusses the philosophizing of his melancholy courtier Jaques (i), who is being made even more than usually morose by the singing of another courtier, Amiens (v). When the Duke meets him, however, Jaques is now merry, having met the clever fool, Touchstone, in the forest (vii). Meanwhile Orlando has been desperately searching for food (vi); now with drawn sword he enters the Duke's banqueting place and demands food. But the Duke meets him with unexpected kindness and welcomes him as Sir Rowland's son (vii).

**ACT III.** Back at the court, Duke Frederick has told Oliver that if he cannot find his brother he will lose all his estates (i). While this is going on, Orlando is wandering through the forest, hanging love verses to Rosalind upon the branches of trees. Rosalind finds the verses, and finally, still in her disguise, she talks with the despondent Orlando. As "Ganymede" she offers to pose as Rosalind and to allow Orlando to practice his wooing with her (ii). While Touchstone is planning his own romance (iii), Rosalind laments that Orlando has not come to her as he had promised (iv). Now, still disguised as "Ganymede" she witnesses the love affair of Phebe and Silvius, two shepherds. Phebe treats her swain coldly and "Ganymede" chides her for it, but Phebe instantly falls in love with "Ganymede." When Rosalind ("Ganymede") leaves, Phebe says that she will write the youth a letter and that Silvius must bear it (v).

**ACT IV.** Orlando practices wooing the disguised Rosalind (i); Jaques talks with hunters in the forest (ii); Silvius delivers Phebe's letter (iii). Now a chastened Oliver finds Rosalind. While sleeping in a forest, he tells her, he was saved from the attack of a lioness by his brother Orlando. Orlando has been wounded and Oliver bears a bloody napkin as a token of the fight. Rosalind swoons, then pretends that she has been counterfeiting (iii).

**ACT V.** Orlando and Oliver are now reconciled, and Oliver tells his brother that he has fallen in love with "Aliena," the disguised Celia. They will be married, he says, the next day. Orlando moons for his Rosalind, but "Ganymede" comforts him. She is, she says, a magician; and if Oliver marries "Aliena," Orlando will marry Rosalind. She also promises rather ambiguously to solve the love problems of the shepherd and shepherdess. Phebe promises to marry Silvius if she decides not to marry "Ganymede" (ii). Touchstone, meanwhile, is continuing his romance with Audrey (i, iii). At last Rosalind reveals her true identity. Phebe, who, of course, cannot marry the now nonexistent Ganymede, promises to marry Silvius. Jaques de Boys, brother of Oliver and Orlando, now comes with the news that Duke Frederick, who has been converted and has forsworn the world, has restored his brother, the banished Duke, to his estates. Rosalind recites an epilogue (iv).

# TWELFTH NIGHT; OR, WHAT YOU WILL

## Cast of Characters

### *Main Characters*

ORSINO, Duke of Illyria, a romantic young man. At first in love with Olivia, he eventually settles his affections on Viola.

SEBASTIAN, Viola's twin brother. When Viola is dressed as a young man, she and Sebastian are often mistaken for each other.

SIR TOBY BELCH, Olivia's roistering uncle. In the Falstaff tradition Sir Toby is always looking for a gull; and, except for one instance, when in a tight place he invariably lands on his feet.

SIR ANDREW AGUECHEEK, the perfect fool and gull. Sir Toby uses him as his bank by promising to win him Olivia's hand.

MALVOLIO, Olivia's humorless steward. Although Malvolio has sometimes been played as a heavy, semitragic character, Shakespeare obviously intends him as a comic butt.

OLIVIA, a rich countess and a comparatively colorless character when viewed in relation to Viola. Orsino falls in love with her; she, in turn, falls in love with the disguised Viola; then, thinking that Sebastian is Viola, she induces him to marry her.

VIOLA, one of Shakespeare's famous women. Sweet and dependent by nature, she meets the difficulties of her situation with courage. She falls in love with Orsino and eventually wins him.

MARIA, Olivia's maid. A sharp, but essentially kindly woman, she confounds Malvolio with her plot. Eventually she wins Sir Toby.

### *Supporting Characters*

ANTONIO, a sea captain and associate of Sebastian

FABIAN
FESTE, a clown } servants to Olivia

A SEA CAPTAIN, who befriends Viola

VALENTINE and CURIO, gentlemen attending on the Duke

(Lords, Priests, Sailors, Officers, Musicians, and other Attendants)

(Place: *A city in Illyria, and the seacoast near it*)

BACKGROUND. Performed in 1600, *Twelfth Night* was not printed until the First Folio in 1623. The sources are comparatively obscure, but the play is probably based on two tales in *Barnabe Riche, his Farewell to Military Profession* (1581). The first of these is "Apolonius and Silla," the second, "Of Two Brethren and their Wives." Riche's source was either Belleforest or Bandello.

## ACT BY ACT ANALYSIS

**ACT I.** Duke Orsino has been besieging the beautiful Olivia for her hand in marriage; she, however, refuses every plea of his emissaries. Ostensibly she refuses because she is in mourning for her brother (i). Meanwhile, Viola and a sea captain, who have been rescued from a shipwreck, land on the coast of Illyria; and Viola believes that her twin brother, Sebastian, has been lost in the wreck. Viola, defenseless, determines to disguise herself as a young man and to seek service with Orsino, who she hears is noble and generous (ii). Under the name of Cesario, she gains Orsino's favor; and, although she falls in love with Orsino herself, she consents to become his go-between with Olivia (iv). In Olivia's household the only retainer who seems to enjoy the enforced mourning for Olivia's brother is the humorless and egotistical Malvolio (v). Sir Toby Belch and his gull, Sir Andrew Aguecheek, both enjoy carousing, aided and abetted by Maria. Sir Toby is keeping his hand in Sir Andrew's pocket by promising to win Olivia for Sir Andrew (iii). Cesario (Viola) arrives to carry "his" master's pleas to Olivia; but to complicate matters, Olivia feels herself falling in love with the pseudo-page. After Cesario leaves, she sends her own ring to "him," pretending that "he" has lost it in her presence, so that "he" will be sure to return to her (v).

**ACT II.** When Cesario receives the ring from Olivia's messenger, "he" realizes and deplores that Olivia is in love with "him" (ii). Sir Toby and Sir Andrew get drunk late at night. Maria enters and begs them to be more quiet; but when Malvolio comes in and reprimands them (including Maria) for their drunkenness, he seals his own doom: they determine to be revenged on him (**iii**). They forge a note which appears to have been sent by Olivia to a lover; when Malvolio receives it, he is sure that he is that lover. The note instructs him to "be opposite with a kinsman, surly with servants"; to wear yellow hose; to go cross-gartered; and to smile continually in Olivia's presence (**v**). Meanwhile, two events have occurred: (1) the presumably dead Sebastian turns up in Illyria with Antonio, a sea captain (**i**); (2) Orsino requests Cesario to carry a further message to Olivia (**iv**).

**ACT III.** When Cesario arrives at Olivia's house, Olivia openly tells "him" that she loves "him"; but Cesario must, of course, ignore Olivia's advances (**i**). Meanwhile, the plot against Malvolio works to perfection: his strange antics in following the injunctions of the note cause him to be imprisoned in a dark room as insane (**ii, iv**). Sir Toby, making more mischief, foments a duel between Sir Andrew and Cesario, on the pretext that the page is a rival suitor for Olivia's hand. As the two unwilling duelists prepare to fight, Antonio rushes in and, believing that Cesario is Sebastian, prevents the duel; however, when officers seize Antonio as a former enemy to Illyria, he asks Cesario, whom he supposes to be Sebastian, for the purse which he has given the young man earlier in the day (**iii, iv**). Upon Cesario's natural denial that "he" knows Antonio, the good captain's faith in human nature is shaken. However, Cesario, upon reflection, realizes that the name *Sebastian* has been spoken; and "he" hopes that "his" brother may be alive (**iv**).

**ACT IV.** Convinced that Cesario is a coward, Sir Andrew rushes out to challenge the page; but instead of Cesario he finds Sebastian. Olivia's entrance prevents Sir Andrew from getting hurt. She, also believing Sebastian to be Cesario, desires him to grant her an interview (**i**). The clown Feste, pretending to be Sir Topas the Parson, baits Malvolio in his prison; then assuming his natural voice, Feste offers to obtain some paper and ink for the prisoner (**ii**). Olivia now convinces the not-unwilling Sebastian that he should marry her (**iii**).

**ACT V.** The Duke and Cesario arrive before Olivia's home, where they meet Antonio. When Antonio again reproaches

Cesario—whom he still believes to be Sebastian—the Duke is completely baffled by Antonio's insistence that the young man has just arrived in Illyria. Olivia enters and speaks in loving accents to Cesario. Orsino is naturally angry at what he supposes has been Cesario's treacherous attempt to win Olivia's affection; but when a priest swears that he has recently married the couple, Orsino becomes furious. Sir Andrew and Sir Toby, meanwhile, have inadvertently picked a fight with Sebastian (believing him to be Cesario) and both enter wounded and bleeding. However, when Sebastian appears almost immediately, all the principals realize that they have been dealing with two persons. Matches are made all around: Sir Toby has married Maria because she has invented the plot against Malvolio; Orsino offers to marry Viola. Everyone is happy except poor Malvolio, who vows revenge on the whole group (i).

# ALL'S WELL THAT ENDS WELL

## Cast of Characters

### Main Characters

BERTRAM, the young Count of Rousillon, proves a cold, faithless husband, and a tricky liar before he sees the light.

HELENA DE NARBON goes to great lengths of trickery herself in order to win her husband, substituting herself for Bertram's mistress in a midnight tryst.

PAROLLES, "a very tainted fellow," is a bad influence upon his young master, Bertram, but his calumnies catch up with him.

DIANA CAPILET, helps Helena secure her husband by grossly deceiving Bertram.

THE WIDOW CAPILET, Diana's mother, also helps in the plot to secure Bertram for Helena.

THE COUNTESS OF ROUSILLON, though she loves her son, cannot approve of the way he treats Helena.

THE KING OF FRANCE is cured by Helena and proves his gratitude.

LAFEU, an old lord, almost succeeds in marrying his daughter to Bertram.

### Supporting Characters

DUKE OF FLORENCE

TWO FRENCH LORDS

LAVACHE, a clown, servant to the Countess Rousillon

MARIANA, neighbor of the Widow Capilet

A PAGE

STEWARD, servant to the Countess Rousillon

VIOLENTA, neighbor of the Widow Capilet

(Lords, Officers, Soldiers, French and Florentine)

(Place: *Rousillon, Paris, Florence, and Marseilles*)

BACKGROUND. This play is probably one recast by Shakespeare about 1601 after being originally written considerably earlier. The earliest printed version is that of the First Folio of 1623. The source for the main plot is William Painter's *Palace of Pleasure* (1566), which is in turn based on a novel from Boccaccio's *Decameron.*

## ACT BY ACT ANALYSIS

**ACT I.** Bertram, the young Count of Rousillon, departs for the King's court, leaving behind his mother and Helena, his mother's ward. Helena is the daughter of a famous physician, now dead, and has been left in the Countess' care. Though she feels that she is hopelessly beneath him, Helena loves Bertram (**i**). While Bertram is being received cordially by the King (**ii**), Helena confesses her love to the Countess. She also unfolds a plan. The King is suffering from an ulcer which has been pronounced incurable by all the doctors in the country, but Helena possesses a wonderful medicine to treat the condition. She now proposes to go to Paris to see the King, and at the same time to be near Bertram (**iii**).

**ACT II.** When Helena arrives and proposes to cure the King, he at first objects; but he finally accepts her treatment on condition that she will forfeit her life if it fails. As a reward, if the cure is successful, she may ask the favor of choosing any husband she wishes (**i**). The King is cured, and when he summons his lords to grant Helena her request, she, of course, chooses Bertram. But Bertram will have none of her. Though the King forces him to marry her, he immediately plans to run away to fight in the Tuscan wars. Parolles, his rascally follower, agrees with false heartiness to all his master says (**iii**) and is deputized to tell Helena that she will be sent to Rousillon, but that her husband will have none of her (**iv**). Bertram takes his leave from Helena very coldly and departs for Florence, the rogue Parolles accompanying him (**v**).

**ACT III.** The Duke of Florence, who is hard pressed for fighting men (**i**), welcomes Bertram and makes him general of his horse troops (**iii**). Meanwhile the scorned Helena returns sadly to Rousillon. She shows the Countess a letter from Bertram setting forth the impossible conditions under which the young lord will be reconciled to her as a wife. He will never accept her until she has possession of a ring which he has never removed from his finger and until she has conceived a child by him— conditions that seem utterly impossible of fulfillment (ii). Helena, though, has a plan. She slips away from Rousillon, leaving a letter for the Countess (iv), and journeys to Florence as a pilgrim. Outside the city walls she meets the Widow Capilet and her daughter Diana, from whom she learns that Bertram has been busily attempting to seduce the daughter (v). Helena concocts a scheme with the widow. Diana shall lead Bertram on until she secures the ring from his finger. Then she shall make an appointment with the faithless husband in her chamber; but at the allotted time, Helena shall substitute herself for Diana in the darkness (vii). Meanwhile a lighter touch has been added by the actions of Parolles. He has made himself unpopular with the Florentine soldiers, who wish to expose him as a coward and rogue. They propose to Bertram that they will test him by pretending to be enemies and capturing the fellow (vi).

**ACT IV.** That night Parolles goes out into the darkness on a mission of pretended danger, planning to stroll about for a time, then to return with a story of wild encounters and deeds of bravery. When the conspiring Florentines seize him, his bubble of bravery instantly collapses (i), and Bertram is allowed to witness his rascally follower's cowardice (iii). But before this occurs, Bertram visits Diana, who secures the ring from him and makes an appointment with him for midnight. During the night, she says, while they are in bed together, she will give him a ring in return (ii). After he has kept the appointment Bertram makes plans to return to France. The war is now over, and he feels that the letters of high recommendation that he bears from the Duke of Florence will soften the King's anger against him. Helena, he is told, is dead (iii), but she is actually arranging to follow her husband to Marseilles where she plans to confront him (iv). Back in Rousillon, Lafeu tells the Countess that Helena is dead. The King, he says, has forgiven Bertram and now plans a marriage between the young man and Lafeu's daughter (v).

**ACT V.** Helena, accompanied by Diana and the widow, not finding Bertram in Marseilles, prepares to follow him to

Rousillon, whence they learn he has gone. Diana sends a letter to precede them (i). The King, his coming announced by Lafeu (ii), arrives at Rousillon and begins to plan the new marriage for Bertram, whom he has forgiven. Lafeu asks for a pledge of faith to give his daughter, and Bertram gives him the ring supplied him by the supposed Diana during their night of love. All are shocked when the ring is recognized as Helena's, given her by the King himself. None of them believes Bertram's flimsy story of how he came by it—he says the ring was thrown to him from a casement window by a noble lady—and the King has Bertram arrested. He is again thoroughly enraged with the young man, even to the point of suspecting him of murdering Helena. Now Diana's letter arrives from Marseilles. In it Diana claims that Bertram has promised to marry her if his wife died; now that this has happened, she demands he make good his promise. Diana follows close upon the heels of the letter and confronts Bertram. Now the youth is forced to confess giving his ring to Diana and accepting a ring in return, but he accuses the girl of being a common camp follower. The King demands that Diana tell where she got Helena's ring—a demand enforced by the threat of death if she refuses to tell. Diana answers that her mother will give her bail, and the widow enters with Helena. She has fulfilled Bertram's impossible demands, and the now thoroughly chastened youth begs her forgiveness. The King brings the action to a close, reciting an epilogue stating that "All is well ended" (iii).

# MEASURE FOR MEASURE

## Cast of Characters

### Main Characters

VINCENTIO, Duke of Venice, an admirable, kindly ruler, but so afraid of being thought a tyrant that he refuses to accept the responsibility for enforcing the harsh laws of his country.

ANGELO, Vincentio's deputy, a hard and frosty man, cannot himself resist temptation. He falls into the very sin he punishes others for.

CLAUDIO, a young gentleman, nearly loses his life because of his unrestrained love.

ISABELLA, Claudio's sister, refuses to sacrifice her honor for her brother's life, and turns from a nunnery to marry the Duke.

MARIANA, once engaged to Angelo and spurned by him, helps in a plot which finally finds her married to the hard-hearted deputy.

JULIET, Claudio's sweetheart, suffers many indignities before her lover finally becomes her husband.

### Supporting Characters

ABHORSON, an executioner

BARNARDINE, a prisoner

ELBOW, a stupid constable

ESCALUS, an old lord

FRANCISCA, a nun

FROTH, a silly gentleman

LUCIO, another foolish gentleman

MISTRESS OVERDONE, a prostitute

PETER, a friar

POMPEY, a servant

PROVOST, a jailer

THOMAS, a friar

VARRIUS, a gentleman attending on the Duke

(Gentlemen, a Justice, Lords, Officers, a Boy, Attendants)

(Place: *The city of Vienna*)

BACKGROUND. Composed and performed in 1604, the play was not printer until 1623. A play by George Whetstone, *Promos and Cassandra* (1578), furnishes the direct source. Whetstone's play is in turn based upon an incident from the *Hecatommithi* (1565), a work by the Italian writer, Giraldi Cinthio. Cinthio is thought to have drawn his tale from an actual occurrence in an Italian town. Though the play is usually classed among the comedies, it has been called a "problem play." Its dark and brooding tragic overtones are relieved only by a happy ending.

## ACT BY ACT ANALYSIS

**ACT I.** Unwilling to enforce the harsh laws of his domain, the Duke of Vienna announces his plans to leave the city for a time. In his absence, he appoints Angelo to rule, aided by Escalus (**i**). The Duke, however, merely goes into hiding disguised as a friar, making Friar Thomas his confidant (**iii**). As soon as he assumes power, Angelo arrests Claudio for sexual promiscuity with Juliet, the girl Claudio plans to marry. Unable to find the Duke and appeal directly for mercy, the unfortunate young man sends Lucio to find Isabella, Claudio's sister. She is about to enter a nunnery, but Claudio hopes that she will delay her entrance long enough to intercede for him (**ii**). When Isabella receives the message, she promises to plead with Angelo (**iv**). Meanwhile, throughout the act the effect of Angelo's law enforcement campaign upon the lower strata of the city's society is illustrated by the actions of Elbow, the foolish constable, who pursues Madame Overdone and her servant, the clown Pompey.

**ACT II.** Escalus appeals to Angelo on behalf of Claudio. The stern deputy refuses to be lenient and justifies his harshness on the grounds that an example must be made (**i**). Now Isabella appears and adds her pleas to those of Escalus. Still unmoved, Angelo does, however, consent to see her again on the following day. Left alone, Angelo wonders aloud if his own motives concerning Isabella are honorable (**ii**). Next day Isabella returns.

His passion thoroughly aroused, Angelo offers to free her brother if she will submit to him. Refusing, she threatens to expose him; he scoffs; no one, he says, will believe her story. Utterly crushed, she realizes that he has spoken truly (**iv**).

**ACT III.** Awaiting his execution, Claudio receives Isabella, who tells him of Angelo's proposal. Panicky at the thought of approaching death, Claudio pleads with his sister to accept Angelo's offer; but soon he realizes the enormity of his conduct. In his role as a sympathetic friar, the Duke suggests a counter-plot. He suggests that the sister accept Angelo's monstrous proposition. But Mariana, a girl who was once engaged to marry Angelo, and who still loves him, will be substituted when the assignation takes place (**i**). On the comic level, Elbow continues his pursuit of Madam Overdone and her entourage, and finally succeeds in having them imprisoned. Lucio entertains the disguised Duke with tall tales of the Duke's supposed misdemeanors, supposing that he is impressing a simple friar (**ii**).

**ACT IV.** Mariana agrees (offstage) to take Isabella's place "i' th' dark," and the meeting with Angelo is arranged (**i**). Angelo suspects nothing when he meets her; but instead of freeing Claudio, he treacherously sends his jailer a letter confirming the execution and demands that Claudio's head be sent to him. At first the disguised Duke and the jailer plan to substitute the head of Barnardine, a condemned criminal (**ii**); but finally they decide to spare him and send the head of an already dead pirate. Now the Duke is ready to spring his trap for Angelo. He writes a note telling his deputy that he plans to return, and arranges to be met at the city gates (**iii**). He plots with Isabella: she is to accuse Angelo of deflowering her. Mariana, the real victim, is to play another role (**iv**).

**ACT V.** Isabella denounces Angelo, who denies his guilt. The Duke, now stripped of his disguise, pretends to defend the guilty deputy, and sends for his other self (the friar) to plead the women's cause. He leaves the stage and returns again disguised. At a properly dramatic moment, the poor friar is revealed as the real ruler of the city. When Angelo, confronted by his master, confesses, he is forced to marry Mariana. Once married, he is sentenced to death but is finally spared when it is revealed that Claudio still lives. Claudio and Juliet are reunited, and the Duke announces his love for Isabella. Tripped up by his earlier bragging and lying, Lucio is forced to marry a prostitute (i).

# PERICLES, PRINCE OF TYRE

## Cast of Characters

### *Main Characters*

PERICLES, Prince of Tyre, undergoes many journeys and troubles before he is reunited with his wife and daughter.

THAISA, daughter of Simonides and wife of Pericles, finally leaves the temple of Diana to join her husband and daughter.

MARINA, Pericles' lost daughter, survives a murder attempt and manages to maintain her virtue even in a brothel.

ANTIOCHUS, king of Antioch, whose incestuous relationship with his daughter is discovered by Pericles in a riddle.

HELICANUS is chosen to rule Tyre in Pericles' absence.

SIMONIDES, king of Pentapolis and Pericles' father-in-law.

CLEON, governor of Tarsus, is shocked by his wife's supposed murder of Marina, but makes no attempt to punish her for it.

DIONYZA, Cleon's wife, attempts to murder the child she has promised to protect and rear.

LYSIMACHUS, governor of Mytilene, cannot possess Marina in a brothel, but finally possesses her as a wife.

CERIMON, a lord of Ephesus, through his potent medicines, revives the dead queen Thaisa.

BOULT, the Pandar's servant, after attempting to ravish Marina, finally decides to help her.

### *Supporting Characters*

A BAWD, the wife of the Pandar  
THE DAUGHTER OF ANTIOCHUS  
DIANA, the goddess  
ESCANES, a lord of Tyre  
GOWER, as chorus  
LEONINE, a servant, commissioned to murder Marina  

LYCHORIDA, Marina's nurse  
MARSHAL  
PANDAR, a whoremaster  
PHILEMON, Cerimon's servant  
THALIARD, commissioned by Antiochus to murder Pericles

(Lords, Ladies, Knights, Gentlemen, Sailors, Pirates, Fishermen, and Messengers)

(Place: *Tyre, Tarsus, Pentapolis, Mytilene, Ephesus and the temple of Diana there, Shipboard between Pentapolis and Tarsus and off Mytilene*)

BACKGROUND. *Pericles* was first published in a very corrupt quarto edition in 1609 but was not included in either the First Folio edition of 1623 or the second of 1632. The work was probably first composed and presented in 1607 or 1608. Most scholars agree that *Pericles* is only partly the work of Shakespeare and most agree in assgining him the last three acts. The play is a dramatization of the story *Apolonius of Tyre,* a very well-known literary theme.

## ACT BY ACT ANALYSIS

**ACT I.** Each of the acts and some of the scenes are introduced by an actor representing Gower, the English poet, who presents an epilogue together with (in some cases) a dumb show. Antiochus, king of Antioch, has given prospective suitors for the hand of his daughter a riddle to solve. Those who fail to solve the riddle must die. Pericles comes to try the riddle and from it he discovers that Antiochus is engaged in an incestuous relationship with his daughter. Knowing that Antiochus will not willingly let him live after he has guessed this, Pericles flees back to Tyre. He has guessed rightly; for Antiochus immediately appoints Thaliard, an Antiochan lord, to murder Pericles. Finding his quarry flown, Antiochus sends Thaliard after the departed prince (**i**). Arrived safely in Tyre, Pericles fears some such plot as Antiochus has planned. Helicanus—one of Pericles' lords whom he takes into his confidence—fears the same thing and suggests that Pericles go traveling until Antiochus has lost his rage or is reported dead. Leaving his government in the hands of Helicanus (**ii**), Pericles departs ahead of Thaliard, who plans to tell Antiochus that Pericles has perished at sea (**iii**). Pericles lands at poverty-stricken Tarsus, bringing provisions to relieve the distressed inhabitants, an act for which Cleon, the governor, is highly grateful (**iv**).

**ACT II.** Here Pericles tarries for a time, and a grateful people erect a statue in his honor. But when a messenger brings news of Thaliard's visit to Tyre, Pericles believes it dangerous to

stay longer in Tarsus, and journeys on to Pentapolis where he
loses his fleet in a shipwreck and barely manages to stagger
ashore alive. He learns that the king of Pentapolis, Simonides,
is planning a tourney for the hand of his daughter; and after
rescuing his armor from the nets of the fishermen whom he
meets upon the shore, Pericles plans to enter the tourney (i).
After passing in review before the king and his daughter (ii),
Pericles wins the tourney and attends a banquet, at which it
becomes evident that Thaisa, the daughter, thinks highly of him
(iii). After pretending anger that such a penniless fellow should
presume to court his daughter (an act which Pericles, fearing
reprisals from the king, denies) Simonides joins the hands of
the young couple in marriage (v). Meanwhile, back in Tyre,
news has reached the court that Antiochus and his daughter
have both died. The Tyrean lords, not knowing whether
Pericles is alive or dead, wish to appoint Helicanus king. But
Helicanus insists that they search for their missing lord for
another year before they take such a step (iv).

**ACT III.** Gower tells us in the prologue that Pericles has married
the beautiful Thaisa and that she is with child. When he
receives a message telling him of the state of affairs in Tyre and
the necessity of his immediate return, he leaves for home,
accompanied by his wife. In a storm at sea Thaisa gives birth
to a daughter but dies during her delivery, and is buried at sea
in a well-caulked coffin. Since they are near Tarsus, Pericles
runs for this port, since he thinks his newborn daughter cannot
survive the long journey back to Tyre (i). But in Ephesus there
lives one Cerimon, uncannily skilled in medicine, and when the
dead queen's coffin floats ashore here, Cerimon revives her (ii).
Since Thaisa despairs of ever seeing Pericles again, she leaves
the world and enters a temple of Diana as a priestess (iv).
Pericles, who has in the meantime reached Tarsus safely, leaves
his daughter, whom he names Marina for her sea birth, with his
friend Cleon, while he sails back to Tyre to reclaim his throne
(iii).

**ACT IV.** Left in the care of Cleon and his wife, Marina grows
into such a beautiful girl, so skilled in all the arts, that she
quite eclipses Philoten, Cleon's daughter. Dionyza, Philoten's
mother, in a fury of jealousy, plans to murder Marina and

commissions a servant, Leonine, to do the deed. But before the fellow can commit the act, Marina is seized by pirates who carry her away (i) to Mytilene, where they sell her to a brothel keeper, who immediately has his servant sent to cry this new virgin ware upon the streets (ii). Back in Tarsus, Dionyza confesses her evil deed to her husband, who, though he does not condone the act, makes no attempt to punish his wife (iii). They build a monument to the girl which Gower and a dumb show reveal as having been visited by the grief-stricken father, who puts on sackcloth and makes hermit's vows as he returns to his ship. Far from dead, Marina is actually preaching divinity in the brothel (v). The governor, who comes disguised to the brothel, is struck by the beauty and innocence of the girl and gives her gold without making any other advances. Even Boult, the pander's villainous servant, who is given permission by his master to ravish the stubborn girl, is moved by her pleas (and the gold she gives him). She persuades him to remove her from the brothel and install her as a teacher of the fine arts in a decent household (vi).

**ACT V.** Gower tells us that Marina succeeds in her purpose and is installed as a teacher—an occupation by which she is earning a good deal of money for her master, the pander. Pericles, who in his grief refuses to speak to anyone, now visits Mytilene, and Lysimachus puts off in his barge to the Prince's ship. Upon being told of Pericles' affliction, Lysimachus suggests that Marina, who is so skilled in gentle ways, be brought in an attempt to cheer Pericles. She comes, tells Pericles her story; and he recognizes his daughter. The joyous father, hearing the music of the spheres, falls asleep and sees a vision of the goddess Diana, who tells him to visit her temple at Ephesus (i). After granting Lysimachus the hand of Marina upon his return from Ephesus, Pericles goes to the temple (ii). Here he tells his story to the assembled votaresses, and Thaisa faints when she hears it. A joyous reunion is effected, and Gower brings an epilogue telling us that we have witnessed the triumph of virtue and the defeat of vice. Antiochus and his daughter, he says, have been struck down and Cleon and his daughter killed by their own people when their deed became public (iii).

# CYMBELINE

## Cast of Characters

### *Main Characters*

CYMBELINE, King of Britain, a weak man, easily swayed by his evil Queen.

CLOTEN, the Queen's son by a former husband. Though he is a doltish lout, he is not without some patriotism. His mother is intent on his marrying Imogen.

POSTHUMUS LEONATUS, a gentleman, Imogen's husband. In our day Posthumus' wager with Iachimo seems to be in poor taste; however, to the Renaissance mind it probably was a perfectly honest act of faith in Imogen.

IACHIMO, the villain. Note the similarity between his name and Iago's in *Othello*. In general, he is the same kind of scheming opportunist; but his plans fail, and he is saved from death.

QUEEN, Cymbeline's wife. She is an example of the traditional stepmother. Anxious to advance Cloten, she is completely unscrupulous in her methods.

IMOGEN, Cymbeline's daughter by a former marriage. She is one of Shakespeare's triumphs of characterization: though faithful and loving, she is capable of desperate measures when they become necessary.

### *Supporting Characters*

ARVIRAGUS, son of Cymbeline, disguised under the name of Cadwal

BELARIUS, a banished lord disguised under the name of Morgan

CAIUS LUCIUS, emissary for Augustus Caesar and general of the Roman forces which invade Britain

CORNELIUS, a physician

GUIDERIUS, son of Cymbeline, disguised under the name of Polydore

PHILARIO, friend of Posthumus, who introduces Posthumus to Iachimo

PISANIO, servant of Posthumus

(A Roman Captain; two British Captains; a Frenchman, friend of Philario; two Lords of Cymbeline's court; two Gentlemen of the same; two Gaolers; HELEN, a lady attending on Imogen; Lords Ladies; Roman Senators; Tribunes; a Soothsayer; a Dutchman; a Spaniard; Musicians; Officers; Captains; Soldiers; Messengers; Attendants; Apparitions)

(Place: *Britain; Rome*)

BACKGROUND. *Cymbeline* was probably composed and played in 1610. The first appearance in print is in the First Folio of 1623. Some critics claim to see the hand of an interpolator or collaborator, especially with regard to the verse of Posthumus' vision. The two principal sources are a tale from the second day of the *Decameron* by Boccaccio and Holinshed's *Chronicle*. Shakespeare may also have received some ideas from a play printed in 1589, *The Rare Triumphs of Love and Fortune*.

## ACT BY ACT ANALYSIS

**ACT I.** Cymbeline, King of Britain, has married a second wife, a widow with one son, Cloten. The Queen, to protect the interests of her son, wishes him to marry Imogen, daughter of Cymbeline and heiress apparent to the throne. However, her plans hit a snag when Imogen marries Posthumus, a noble gentleman, who because of his family's bravery in the service of Cymbeline, has been reared at court. Posthumus has been a great favorite with the King, partly because Cymbeline's own sons, Guiderius and Arviragus, have been kidnaped in infancy. The Queen succeeds in arousing the King's anger at Posthumus and Imogen because of their hasty marriage and convinces him that he should banish the young bridegroom from court, though she pretends to be friendly to the lovers. As Imogen and Posthumus part, she gives him a ring and receives a bracelet in return (i). When Posthumus prepares to leave the court for exile in Italy, the doltish Cloten draws his sword on him; but they are parted before Cloten is hurt (i, ii). The only person left at court to comfort the distracted Imogen is Pisanio, Posthumus' faithful servant (iii). When Posthumus arrives in Rome and sings the praises of his wife in the company of Iachimo, the latter challenges Imogen's chastity. A wager is then proposed: Iachimo is to go to Britain and test Imogen's faithfulness; if he brings back proof of his intimacy with her, he will receive Posthumus' ring and friendship; if not, he must pay Posthumus ten thousand ducats and fight a duel with him (**iv**). Iachimo arrives at the British court and attempts to seduce Imogen with a story of Posthumus' unfaithfulness to her; but when she refuses to believe the lie, Iachimo dissembles, says that he has been testing her, and asks her to keep a trunk full of treasure for him in her room. She willingly consents (**vi**). Meanwhile, the Queen has made plans to rid herself of Imogen by putting what she thinks is a deadly poison in the hand of Pisanio with instructions to deliver it as a cordial to Imogen; however, Cornelius, the physician, has mixed, instead of a poison, a harmless sleeping potion (**v**).

**ACT II.** As Imogen retires, Iachimo, who has hidden in the trunk, approaches her, observes the chamber closely, slips the bracelet off her arm, notices a mole on her left breast, and returns to the trunk (**ii**). When he returns to Rome, he describes these details and shows the bracelet to Posthumus. The husband believes his wife guilty (**iv**) and delivers a diatribe on the weakness of women (**v**). Meanwhile, Cloten is angered by Imogen's contemptuous treatment of his suit for her hand and swears revenge (**iii**).

**ACT III.** Pisanio receives a letter from Posthumus, requesting him to kill Imogen. Imogen also receives a letter from Posthumus, which requests her to accompany Pisanio to Wales ostensibly to meet him there, actually to afford Pisanio an opportunity to kill her (**ii**). When the two arrive in Wales, Pisanio, unable to fulfill his master's request, shows her the letter. He suggests that she dress as a boy; and, since Lucius, the Roman ambassador is to arrive in Wales shortly, he advises her to accompany the Romans to Italy, to find Posthumus, and to make her peace with him (**iv**). Imogen, lost, wanders around the Welsh hills and seeks refuge in a cave. This cave is inhabited by three mountaineers (identified in **iii** as Belarius, Guiderius, and Arviragus). Belarius, a nobleman, having been misjudged by Cymbeline, out of revenge has kidnaped the Kings' sons in infancy and has raised them under assumed names as his own sons. When the three return to the cave, the boys feel un-accountably attracted to the disguised Imogen (**vi**). Meanwhile, Lucius, who has come to Britain to collect tribute for Augustus Caesar, is refused the tribute by Cymbeline, who has been egged on by the Queen and Cloten (**i**). The Romans consequently plan to invade Britain (**vii**). Pisanio, now that Imogen is safe, saves his own life by showing to Cloten Imogen's letter from Posthumus and by giving Cloten some of Posthumus' clothes. Cloten now intends to ambush Posthumus when he comes to Wales and to ravish Imogen (**v**).

**ACT IV.** In Wales, Belarius sees Cloten and recognizes him. Under provocation Guiderius kills Cloten and cuts off his head. Meanwhile Imogen has taken the cordial and lies seemingly dead in the cave. Guiderius and Arviragus place her body with honors beside Cloten's headless trunk. She awakens, sees the corpse dressed in Posthumus' garments, and believes it to be her husband. Sick at heart, she meets Lucius and the Romans, tells them that the dead man is her master, watches him buried, and goes with Lucius as his page (**ii**). Meanwhile, things are going badly with Cymbeline: his Queen is mortally ill; Cloten and Imogen are missing; and the Romans are on their way to Britain (**iii**). In spite of the misgivings of Belarius, he yields to the pleas of Guiderius and Arviragus, and he and the boys decide to fight for Britain against the Romans (**iv**).

**ACT V.** Posthumus has received a bloody handkerchief from Pisanio; and, believing it to be a token of Imogen's death, he is struck with remorse. He had come to Britain with the Romans, but now intends to disguise as a British peasant and to fight for Britain (**i**). Posthumus, Belarius, Guiderius, and Arviragus are the heroes of the battle: they rally the Britons, who have been in retreat. In single combat with Iachimo, Posthumus disarms him, but leaves him alive (**ii**). The day won, Posthumus longs for death; he displays himself as a Roman before the Britons and is taken prisoner (**iii**). In prison under sentence of death, Posthumus sees a vision, in which Jupiter prophesies that when a lion's whelp shall be embraced by a piece of tender air and when from a stately cedar lopped branches shall be jointed to the old stock and revive, then shall Posthumus be happy and Britain fortunate. A messenger enters and orders Posthumus to be unshackled and to be taken to the King (**iv**). Meanwhile, the Queen has died, and Cornelius enters with her confession of her villainies: she has intended to murder Cymbeline himself. Imogen, still disguised as a boy, is brought in with the Roman prisoners, and Lucius begs for her life. Cymbeline feels that he has seen the pseudo-boy before, and the three mountaineers are struck with wonder at seeing the one who they have thought was dead. When Cymbeline offers to grant her a boon, she asks Iachimo, also among the prisoners, whence he has received the ring he is wearing. Iachimo confesses his guilt, and in turn Cornelius tells his story of the supposed poison which he furnished the Queen. Imogen is thereupon restored to her father and to her husband. When Guiderius confesses his murder of Cloten, the three mountaineers stand under penalty of death until Belarius confesses his kidnaping; then the sons are restored to their father. The soothsayer now interprets Posthumus' vision: Posthumus Leonatus (*leo-natus*) is the lion's whelp; the tender air (*mulier* supposedly from *mollis aer*) is Imogen; the lofty cedar is Cymbeline, and the lost branches are his sons. Everyone, even Iachimo, is forgiven; Cymbeline is to resume his tribute to Rome; and Rome and Britain are to live in peace (**v**).

# THE WINTER'S TALE

## Cast of Characters

### Main Characters

LEONTES, King of Sicilia. His unwarranted jealousy of Hermione precipitates the action of the play.

CAMILLO, Lord of Sicilia. He leaves Leontes' service for that of Polixenes when Leontes orders him to kill Polixenes. He remains the faithful friend of all the principal characters.

POLIXENES, King of Bohemia. Leontes suspects that Polixenes has cuckolded him. Then Polixenes' opposition to his son's marriage to Perdita brings the action back to Sicilia.

FLORIZEL, son of Polixenes and Prince of Bohemia, in love with Perdita.

HERMIONE, Leontes' Queen, unjustly suspected of infidelity. In a simple yet effective courtroom speech, she stoutly maintains her innocence.

PERDITA, daughter of Leontes and Hermione, in love with Florizel. The discovery of her identity fulfills the prophecy of the Delphic oracle.

PAULINA, wife of Antigonus, sharp-tongued but burning for justice. She acts, in a sense, as Leontes' conscience.

### Supporting Characters

ANTIGONUS, a lord of Sicilia, husband to Paulina. He leaves the infant Perdita in Bohemia and is punished by death for the injustice.

ARCHIDAMUS, a lord of Bohemia

AUTOLYCUS, one of Shakespeare's famous rogues. He cheats the rustics at every opportunity.

CLEOMENES and DION, Lords of Sicilia

MAMILLIUS, young Prince of Sicilia

OLD SHEPHERD, reputed father of Perdita

CLOWN, his son

> (A Mariner; a Gaoler; EMILIA, a lady attending on
> Hermione; MOPSA and DORCAS, Shepherdesses; Time, as
> chorus; other Lords and Gentlemen; Ladies; Officers;
> Servants; Shepherds; and Shepherdesses.)

> (Place: *Sicilia and Bohemia*)

BACKGROUND. Played in 1611, this drama found its way into print
in the First Folio of 1623. The principal source is Robert Greene's
*Pandosto, The Triumph of Time* (1588). There are also some minor
sources.

## ACT BY ACT ANALYSIS

**ACT I.** Polixenes, King of Bohemia, has been visiting at the
court of his boyhood friend Leontes, King of Sicilia (**i**). When
the time arrives for Polixenes to return to Bohemia, Leontes in
vain begs his friend to extend his stay. But Queen Hermione, at
her husband's behest, finally convinces Polixenes that he should
remain a time longer. Now, however, Leontes becomes irration-
ally jealous of Queen Hermione and Polixenes. Positive in his
own mind that Polixenes is cuckolding him and is the father of
Hermione's unborn child, Leontes orders Camillo, Polixenes'
cupbearer at the Sicilian Court, to poison Polixenes. Camillo
pretends to agree to do the deed, but immediately finds Polixenes
and tells him of Leontes' enmity. Polixenes takes Camillo into
his own service and leaves the Sicilian Court by stealth. Meanwhile, of course, Hermione is left to bear the brunt of her
husband's jealousy (**ii**).

**ACT II.** When he hears of Polixenes' departure, Leontes is
furious. In spite of the protests of some of his courtiers, Leontes
separates Hermione from Mamillius, their son, and orders her
to prison. He proposes to hold her in confinement until he hears
from the Delphic oracle the truth about his domestic situation
(**i**). Meanwhile, in prison Hermione gives birth to a daughter.
Paulina determines to carry the child to Leontes, hoping thus
to soften the father's heart (**ii**). But when she delivers the baby
to Leontes, he insists that it is not his child and orders it burned.
Somewhat softened by the horrified exclamations of the

courtiers, he relents to the extent that he pledges Antigonus, Paulina's husband, to take the child abroad by sea and to leave it in some remote and deserted place (iii).

**ACT III.** At the trial of Hermione, Leontes accuses her of adultery. Simply and nobly, she denies the indictment. The oracle from Delphi is then read in the court: it states that "Hermione is chaste; Polixenes blameless; Camillo a true subject; Leontes a jealous tyrant; his innocent babe truly begotten; and the King shall live without an heir, if that which is lost is not found." When Leontes blasphemously denies the validity of the oracle, he is immediately informed that Mamillius has died. To add further catastrophe, Paulina enters with word that Hermione also is dead. Leontes is thus left completely alone (ii). Meanwhile, in a dream Antigonus has been instructed to leave the babe in Bohemia and to name her Perdita. He also dreams that because of his share in Leontes' guilt, he shall never see Paulina again. No sooner has he laid Perdita on the ground than he is chased and killed by a bear, and the ship in which he has come is destroyed by a storm. Perdita is found by a shepherd and his son, a clown. The shepherd, impressed by the clothes of the infant and by the gold left beside her, decides to take her home with him (iii).

**ACT IV.** Sixteen years have elapsed; Perdita has been taught to consider the shepherd her father (i). Polixenes, meanwhile, has received information that his son, Florizel, has been visiting a shepherd's hovel to see the shepherd's pretty daughter. He confers with Camillo, and the two decide to disguise themselves and visit the shepherd so that they may observe Florizel's actions (ii). Since Perdita knows that Florizel is the King's son, she is worried about what will happen when the King discovers that they are in love. Polixenes and Camillo arrive at the shepherd's hut during the sheep-shearing feast. There is much merriment: a dance of shepherds and shepherdesses; a dance of satyrs; singing by Autolycus, a rogue who consistently cheats the clown and the other rustics. When the shepherd announces the engagement of Perdita to Florizel, Polixenes reveals his identity; denounces his son with much bitterness; and threatens the shepherd, the clown, and Perdita with death. Since Florizel has a boat ready to sail, Camillo (who now wishes to return to

Sicilia) suggests that Florizel and Perdita sail for Sicilia and put themselves under Leontes' protection without telling him that they are fleeing from Polixenes. Camillo then intends to inform Polixenes of the flight and thus expects to secure his own return to Sicilia by following the lovers. Meanwhile, to protect himself, the shepherd decides to reveal to Polixenes that Perdita is not his daughter and to show the King the clothes and money which he found lying beside the deserted child. However, on their way to find Polixenes, the shepherd and the clown meet Autolycus, who, hoping to return to the service of the Prince, induces them to go with him on board Florizel's boat (**iv**).

**ACT V.** In Sicilia, Paulina exacts a promise from Leontes that he will never marry again until she can choose a wife for him. Florizel and Perdita, pretending to be married, arrive and receive a gracious welcome from Leontes. Word now comes that Polixenes is also in Sicilia, has met the shepherd and the clown, and intends to find the lovers. Florizel confesses to Leontes that he is not married and that his beloved is of humble birth. Leontes promises to intercede with Polixenes for the lovers (**i**). By report we learn the following news: through the shepherd's story Perdita has been acknowledged the daughter of Leontes; Paulina has discovered Antigonus' death; and Paulina has had created a statue of Hermione. The shepherd and the clown are now made gentlemen for their part in the affair (**ii**). Paulina escorts Leontes and the others to the unveiling of the statue. After Leontes has stared at the statue for several minutes, it comes alive; and Hermione herself descends to her husband's arms. She has been in hiding until her daughter is found. All the families are now reunited; and, since Paulina has lost her husband, Leontes suggests that Camillo marry her (**iii**).

# THE TEMPEST

## Cast of Characters

### Main Characters

ALONSO, King of Naples, accessory to the plot which has deprived Prospero of his dukedom

SEBASTIAN, his brother, also an accessory; he later joins with Antonio in an abortive plot to kill Alonso.

PROSPERO, the rightful Duke of Milan. Having been deprived of his dukedom, Prospero, on the island, devotes himself to magic.

ANTONIO, his brother, who has usurped the dukedom and who foments a plot to replace Alonso with Sebastian as King of Naples.

FERDINAND, son of Alonso. He falls in love with Miranda.

MIRANDA, daughter of Prospero. She loves Ferdinand.

### Supporting Characters

ADRIAN and FRANCISCO, Lords

ARIEL, an airy spirit and servant to Prospero

CALIBAN, a monster, son of the witch Sycorax and unwilling servant of Prospero

GONZALO, an honest old counselor, who has befriended Prospero

STEPHANO, a drunken butler, whom Caliban mistakes for a god and who intends to succeed Prospero as master of the island

TRINCULO, a jester, a member of the plot to kill Prospero

(Master of a Ship; Boatswain; Mariners; the following spirits: Iris, Ceres, Juno, Nymphs, Reapers; Other Spirits attending on Prospero)

(Place: *A ship at sea; an uninhabited island*)

BACKGROUND. Played in 1611, this play is probably the last one written entirely by Shakespeare. The first printing is in the First

Folio of 1623. There are a number of influences traceable in the play, but the primary source is probably a letter written by William Strachey called "A true repertory of the wracke of the *Sea Adventure,* and redemption of Sir Thomas Gates, Knight," not printed until 1625 but in private circulation after its date of composition, July 15, 1610. Two other accounts of the wreck probably influenced Shakespeare: Sylvester Jourdan's *A Discovery of the Bermudas, otherwise called the Isle of Divels* and Strachey's *A True Declaration of the Colonie in Virginia.*

## ACT BY ACT ANALYSIS

**ACT I.** Because the chief interests of Prospero, Duke of Milan, lay in "secret studies" rather than statecraft, twelve years ago he was dispossessed of his dukedom by his brother Antonio, aided by Alonso, King of Naples. Antonio, to gain Alonso's aid, promised tribute and homage to Naples. When Antonio set Prospero and his daughter, Miranda, afloat in a rotten boat, they were saved by the ministrations of Gonzalo, who had put into the boat fresh water, food, clothing, and Prospero's books. The two have landed on an island inhabited only by Caliban, son of the witch Sycorax. By setting Ariel free from a tree where he had been confined by Sycorax, Prospero has gained an instrument by which to implement his deep knowledge of magic. Prospero, meanwhile, has promised Ariel eventual freedom. Although Prospero has taught Caliban to speak and has made much of him, Caliban has attempted to ravish Miranda. As punishment, Prospero has reduced him to menial tasks and has kept him under enchantment (**ii**). As the play opens, a terrible storm founders a ship carrying Alonso, Sebastian, Antonio, Ferdinand, and Gonzalo from the wedding of Alonso's daughter (**i**). This tempest has been raised by Prospero, who intends to gain revenge against his former persecutors. Ariel separates the noble personages from the mariners as they seek refuge on the island; and, careful to save the lives of all of them, he leads Ferdinand, son of Alonso, to Prospero's cell. Although Miranda and Ferdinand are immediately attracted to each other, Prospero charms Ferdinand and sets him at menial tasks; Prospero wishes to be certain that the conquest of his daughter be not easy (**ii**).

**ACT II.** On another part of the island Alonso, Sebastian, Antonio, Gonzalo, and others are glad to escape with their lives;

but Alonso mourns for Ferdinand, whom he believes dead, and the others worry as to how they will be rescued. When Ariel charms all but Antonio and Sebastian to sleep, these two plot the murder of Alonso, intending to supplant him with Sebastian. Ariel awakens the others in time to prevent mischief (**i**). In still another part of the island Caliban meets the drunken Trinculo and Stephano; impressed especially by Stephano and his liquor, Caliban claims him as his master (**ii**).

**ACT III.** Prospero, much pleased, overhears Ferdinand's proposal of marriage to Miranda (**i**). Meanwhile, Caliban proposes to Stephano that while Prospero sleeps, the two, together with Trinculo, surprise Prospero and kill him; they will then be masters of the island. Ariel overhears their plans (**ii**). Ariel, disguised as a harpy, then teases Alonso and the others: he sets a table with food, and when they try to eat, snatches the food away, accusing them of their previous sins. Alonso is overcome with remorse (**iii**).

**ACT IV.** Prospero now makes his peace with Ferdinand and blesses the betrothal of Ferdinand and Miranda by presenting a pageant in which spirits clothed as Iris, Ceres, Juno, and nymphs celebrate the impending nuptials. Suddenly remembering Caliban's plot, Prospero calls Ariel to him. Ariel informs him that he has charmed the conspirators, who, half drunk, have wandered over the island, and have landed in a dirty wallow. When Caliban finally leads them to Prospero's cell, the drunkards discover cheap but glittering apparel and, to Caliban's disgust, forget all about the plot. Ariel and other spirits enter and drive the three roaring around the island (**i**).

**ACT V.** Ariel now leads Alonso, Gonzalo, Sebastian, and Antonio to Prospero's cell where Prospero discloses his identity, reveals Sebastian's and Antonio's abortive plot against Alonso, and demands the restoration of his dukedom. Prospero then shows the company Ferdinand and Miranda playing chess. Alonso, repentant yet overjoyed to find his son alive, blesses the betrothal. Ariel delivers the master and boatswain, who reveal that the boat was not sunk and is now ready to sail. Finally, Ariel drives in Caliban, Stephano, and Trinculo with their gaudy apparel; when the whole company laughs at them,

Caliban cannot understand how he has mistaken these drunkards for gods. Before Prospero accompanies the group into his cell for the night, he sets Ariel free, but instructs him as his last task to furnish calm seas and auspicious winds for the voyage to Naples (i).

# HISTORIES

## OF

# WILLIAM SHAKESPEARE

# THE LIFE AND DEATH OF KING JOHN

## Cast of Characters

### *Main Characters*

KING JOHN, of England, almost loses a kingdom by his plotting.

PHILIP THE BASTARD, illegitimate brother of Robert Faulconbridge, is dubbed Sir Philip Plantagenet as the recognized son of Richard Coeur-de-Lion.

ARTHUR, son of Geoffrey, King John's elder brother, is ordered blinded and murdered by his evil uncle.

QUEEN ELINOR, John's mother, spurs on her son's ambitions.

CONSTANCE, Arthur's mother, perhaps too ambitious for her son, dies shortly after she hears of Arthur's capture by his uncle.

HUBERT DE BURGH cannot bring himself to injure the innocent Arthur.

LEWIS, the Dauphin of France, tries to seize England as Arthur's successor, but fails in the attempt.

BLANCH of Spain, the Dauphin's bride, sees her husband go to war against her uncle on her wedding day.

LYMOGES, Duke of Austria and killer of Richard Coeur-de-Lion. This murder is avenged by Philip, Richard's bastard son.

CARDINAL PANDULPH, a papal legate, excommunicates John, but later welcomes him back to the fold.

| | |
|---|---|
| THE EARL OF ESSEX | desert John for the Dauphin, when |
| THE EARL OF PEMBROKE | they learn of Arthur's death, but |
| THE EARL OF SALISBURY | they finally return to their king. |
| THE LORD BIGOT | |

ROBERT FAULCONBRIDGE, Philip the Bastard's half brother, proves one of John's staunchest defenders against the French.

PHILIP, king of France, almost secures a peace with England before the walls of Angiers.

## Supporting Characters

CHATILLON, Ambassador from France to England

THE EARL OF ESSEX

LADY FAULCONBRIDGE, mother of Robert

JAMES GURNEY, Lady Faulconbridge's servant

PRINCE HENRY, John's son

MELUN, a French lord

PETER OF POMFRET, a prophet

(Lords, Citizens, Sheriff, Heralds, Soldiers, Messengers, Attendants)

(Place: *England and France*)

BACKGROUND. Most editors believe that *King John* was first performed sometime between 1593 and 1596, though no printed form of the play exists before that of the First Folio (1623). The immediate source is an anonymous play, *The Troublesome Raigne of John, King of England*, which was entered in the Stationers' Register in 1591.

## ACT BY ACT ANALYSIS

**ACT I.** King John of England is preparing for war against France. The French ambassador has demanded that he abdicate his throne in favor of Arthur, his nephew, son of his now dead elder brother Geoffrey and Constance of Bretagne. His mother, Queen Elinor, urges him on in his defiance of France. At this time Robert Faulconbridge and his bastard elder brother, Philip, come in litigation over the estate of their father. Philip (usually called The Bastard) is really the son of the mighty Richard Coeur-de-Lion, though if he admits this fact he will lose his claim to the Faulconbridge estate. Despite this, he claims Richard as his parent, and John knights him on the spot as Richard Plantagenet (the family name of John and Richard's line of kings) (**i**).

**ACT II.** The invading English meet the French king and his royal party before the city of Angiers. The king of France is accompanied by his ally, Lymoges, duke of Austria—the slayer of Richard Coeur-de-Lion; and The Bastard immediately begins to insult the killer of his father. The people of Angiers will take no sides in the affair but offer to open their gates if a marriage is arranged between Lewis, the Dauphin (or Crown Prince) of France, and Blanch of Spain, niece of King John— a marriage that will produce peace between the two countries. The marriage is immediately arranged (**i**).

**ACT III.** While Constance is inconsolable about this union of France and Spain—a union which leaves Arthur no chance of gaining the throne of England—Pandulph, a papal legate, arrives to question John about his refusal to admit the Pope's appointed Archbishop of Canterbury to his holy office. John replies arrogantly that England will not submit to any decrees of the Pope. Pandulph's answer is to excommunicate John, and to threaten the King of France with similar treatment if he does not cease his peace negotiations with England (**i**). So the marriage plans come to naught and the armies resume their fighting; The Bastard avenges the death of his father by killing Lymoges, and John captures Arthur (**ii**), who is turned over to Hubert de Burgh with strong hints that he is to be murdered. Then John prepares to retire to England (**iii**). The King of France is worried about the English success at arms and the capture of Arthur, but Pandulph predicts that Arthur will be murdered. Such an event, he says, will smooth the way to the throne of England for the Dauphin, who may make all the claims that Arthur did. England, he adds, is ripe for revolt against John because of John's desecration of the church (**iv**).

**ACT IV.** The cruel John has given Hubert orders that Arthur is to be blinded with hot irons; but Hubert, captivated by the boy's charm and innocence, cannot bring himself to perform the horrid deed. He spares the boy, telling him that he will report his death to the king (**i**). Meanwhile, John has had himself crowned again in a superfluous second ceremony. His advisers warn him to free Arthur, since a rumor that Arthur has been murdered is causing much unrest in the country. When Hubert comes to report the rumor true, the counselors stalk out, accusing John of foul play; and John, true to his nature, turns on Hubert, trying to place all blame for Arthur's death upon him (**ii**). But, unknown to Hubert, Arthur is really dead: killed in an attempt to escape by jumping from the castle wall. His body is discovered by John's counselors—Pembroke, Salisbury, and the Lord Bigot—who are so thoroughly enraged with John that they leave to join the Dauphin against him (**iii**).

**ACT V.** Much to The Bastard's chagrin, John now makes his peace with the Pope through the legate Pandulph, who has promised to call off the French forces. The King is chagrined, too, when The Bastard tells him that Arthur is really dead (Hubert had informed him previously that Arthur was still living), and that the counselors have left to join the enemy, while the people are in wild confusion. The Bastard goes to raise more troops in case the legate cannot make the French desist (**i**). Nor will the persuasion of the legate or the boasting speeches of The Bastard prevent the Dauphin from continuing the fight. Resolutely, he orders his troops forward (**ii**). But, though the battle goes so badly for John that he is forced to leave the field and seek refuge in an abbey, it transpires that because the French have lost a needed supply ship, they are forced to draw back (**iii**). Led by the courageous Faulconbridge, younger brother of The Bastard, the English troops now show such courage that the deserting lords fear that their treachery will overtake them. When a dying French leader brings them word that the French plan to betray them, they return to King John (**iv**). Their absence, together with the loss of the supply ship, dashes the Dauphin's last chance for victory (**v**). But John is not to enjoy his victory. Word comes that he has been poisoned by a monk. The returning lords have brought Prince Henry (John's son) with them (**vi**), and the lords swear allegiance to him as their new king (**vii**).

# THE TRAGEDY OF
# KING RICHARD THE SECOND

## Cast of Characters

### *Main Characters*

KING RICHARD II, reigned 1377-1399. Historically, Richard, son of the Black Prince and grandson of Edward III, gave promise of being a forceful and benevolent ruler. Later he came under the influence of a group of unscrupulous advisers and became extravagant and arbitrary. Because of his heavy taxation, he fell into disfavor with his subjects. The powerful nobles especially resented being replaced in his favor by a group of (in their eyes) wily upstarts. Shakespeare, conscious of Marlowe's *Edward II*, must have realized the suitability of Richard as a tragic protagonist and centered the play on his character, in which a fatal flaw is only too evident.

HENRY BOLINGBROKE, Duke of Hereford, afterwards King Henry IV, reigned 1399-1413. Son of John of Gaunt, and Richard's cousin, he is used by Shakespeare as a foil for Richard. Where Richard is weak and easily influenced, Bolingbroke is strong and capable; where Richard is unrealistic and extreme in both elation and depression, Bolingbroke is quick to face reality and is phlegmatic in temperament; where Richard seems to go out of his way to alienate the people whom he should placate, Bolingbroke is always the adroit politician, capable of dissembling whenever necessary.

JOHN OF GAUNT, Duke of Lancaster, son of Edward III. Shakespeare depicts him as much older than he was historically. Into Gaunt's mouth Shakespeare puts some of the noblest poetry of the tragedy. ( cf. II, i, the speech beginning "This royal throne of kings.") In the first two acts his function is that of Richard's conscience; he constantly prods the king into leaving off his extravagances, which Gaunt believes are ruining the kingdom.

EDMUND OF LANGLEY, Duke of York, fifth son of Edward III. He
acts as Regent of England during Richard's Irish expedition.
Shakespeare depicts him as a fussy old man who attempts to
shame Bolingbroke for marching against his rightful sovereign,
but who is quick to recognize his impotence in quelling the
revolt.

DUKE OF AUMERLE, son of the Duke of York. He adheres to
Richard's party and after Richard's fall joins a plot against
Henry IV.

### Supporting Characters

THOMAS MOWBRAY, Duke of Norfolk, Bolingbroke's antagonist in
the abortive trial by combat. He is commonly thought to have
been instrumental in the murder of Thomas Woodstock, Duke
of Gloucester, sixth son of Edward III.

RICHARD'S PARTY: EARL OF SALISBURY, one of Richard's com-
manders; BUSHY, BAGOT, GREEN, and the EARL OF WILTSHIRE
(who never appears); BISHOP OF CARLISLE, and ABBOT OF
WESTMINSTER, leaders in a plot to restore Richard; SIR
STEPHEN SCROOP; DUKE OF SURREY, a supporter of Aumerle.

HENRY'S PARTY: EARL OF NORTHUMBERLAND, EARL OF WORCES-
TER (who never appears), HENRY PERCY, surnamed Hotspur,
son to Northumberland—the Percy family (cf. *I* and *II Henry
IV*); LORD ROSS; LORD WILLOUGHBY; LORD FITZWATER; SIR
PIERCE OF EXTON, murderer of RICHARD

(LORD BERKLEY; LORD MARSHAL; CAPTAIN of a band of
Welshmen; QUEEN to Richard; DUCHESS OF YORK, mother
of Aumerle; DUCHESS OF GLOUCESTER; Lady attending on
the Queen; Lords; Heralds; Officers; Soldiers; Keeper;
Messenger; Groom; and other Attendants)

(Place:  *England and Wales*)

BACKGROUND. The first record in the Stationers' Register is in
1597, but internal evidence points to 1595 as the year of composition. There were five quartos of this play: 1597, two in 1598,
1608, and 1615. It also appears in the First Folio in 1623. Most
modern texts are based on the first quarto and the First Folio. The
principal source is Holinshed's *Chronicle*.

## ACT BY ACT ANALYSIS

**ACT I.** A smouldering feud has just come into the open.
Bolingbroke accuses Mowbray, first, of having misused the

King's funds; second, of multiple treason; and, third, of having plotted and supervised the murder of the Duke of Gloucester, uncle of Bolingbroke and King Richard. Mowbray defends himself with spirit. Gages are thrown down and picked up, a formal challenge to personal combat. In spite of the efforts of Richard, who obviously enjoys the spotlight, and of old Gaunt, the challengers refuse to take up their own gages. Richard sets Coventry as the place and St. Lambert's Day as the time for the combat (i). Before the combat takes place, some light is thrown on Richard's character in a conversation between Gaunt and the Duchess of Gloucester: Richard has undoubtedly been implicated in the Duke of Gloucester's murder (ii). At Coventry, Richard prevents the combat by throwing down his warder. He banishes Mowbray from England for life and Bolingbroke for ten years (later reduced to six because of Gaunt's sorrow at losing his son) (iii). Somewhat later, when Richard and his advisers hear of the approaching death of Gaunt, they plan as soon as feasible to seize the Lancastrian possessions and to use the funds they thus obtain to carry on the Irish war (iv).

**ACT II.** When Richard appears at Gaunt's bedside, his dying uncle condemns him for listening to flatterers and for wasting the revenues of the realm. Richard, furious, waits for the old man to die and then seizes his estates, which, of course, are Bolingbroke's patrimony. Richard leaves almost immediately for Ireland. Meanwhile, many of the nobles, led by Northumberland, decide to desert Richard, for they have received, word that Bolingbroke is on his way back from France (i). When Bolingbroke arrives in England, so many nobles desert to him that the Duke of York, who is Regent in Richard's absence, is afraid he will be unable to prevent Bolingbroke's advance. The King's friends thus hear nothing but bad news (ii). Bolingbroke and his forces march on Bristol, Bolingbroke constantly reiterating that he has returned only for his birthright. York meets them, calls them rebels, and insists that they disband; but he soon realizes the hopelessness of his situation (iii). Not only the nobles, but also some of the heretofore loyal Welsh soldiers desert Richard's cause (iv).

**ACT III.** The triumphant progress of the rebels continues; they capture and execute Bushy and Green (i). Meanwhile, Richard and Aumerle land in Wales and hear of the rebellion. Aumerle tries in vain to keep up his cousin's spirits under the following successive blows: the Welsh have deserted; the favorites have been executed; and York has given up all effective opposition to Bolingbroke. Richard gives way to despair (ii). Finally, at Flint Castle Richard surrenders to Bolingbroke, who still insists that he wants nothing but his patrimony. Richard is returned to London, a prisoner in all but name (iii). The Queen now hears of Richard's fall (iv).

ACT IV. York informs Bolingbroke that Richard is willing to abdicate. In spite of some opposition from Richard's adherents, who prophesy the Wars of the Roses, Bolingbroke considers himself "drafted" and intends to mount the throne as Henry IV (i).

ACT V. In a touching scene Richard and his Queen part. When he is ordered to Pomfret Castle by Northumberland, Richard prophesies that Henry will eventually turn against the men who have helped him to the throne (i). Meanwhile, the Duke of York discovers that Aumerle is engaged in a plot against Henry. In spite of his Duchess' pleas, York determines to betray the plot to the King (ii). At court, after a passing reference to his "unthrifty son" (cf. *Henry IV* and *Henry V*), Henry receives first Aumerle, then York, and finally the Duchess, who begs for her son's life. After some hesitation Henry accedes to her wishes (iii). Exton has overheard Henry express a wish that he might be rid of Richard; taking the wish literally, Exton intends to fulfill it (iv). Exton murders Richard at Pomfret (v) and brings his body to Henry. The King disclaims any share in the deed, banishes Exton, and determines to go on a crusade to expiate the crime (vi).

# THE FIRST PART OF HENRY THE FOURTH

## Cast of Characters

### *Main Characters*

KING HENRY IV, usurped the throne from his cousin Richard II (cf. *Richard II*). Son of John of Gaunt, he actually has less claim to the throne than Mortimer, who is descended from Lionel, an older son of Edward III. Always the realistic politician, Henry rules England well; but because of his usurpation he is constantly bedeviled by revolts.

HENRY, PRINCE OF WALES. Hal, as he is called, is one of Shakespeare's dynamic character studies. Shakespeare causes King Henry IV to mention him as a wastrel at the close of *Richard II;* and except for one soliloquy (I, ii, 218-240) we see him early in this play as a roisterer with Falstaff and company. Shakespeare is always careful, however, that Hal commit no real crime; his misdeeds always seem to arise from sheer animal spirits. As the play progresses, Hal's sense of responsibility consistently grows (note, for instance, the ever-increasing amount of blank verse that Shakespeare puts into Hal's mouth). Shakespeare carries on this character study in *II Henry IV* and *Henry V*.

THOMAS PERCY, Earl of Worcester, uncle of Hotspur. Cool and rational like the King, Worcester adds to these attributes a cunning which alienates the audience.

HENRY PERCY, Earl of Northumberland, father of Hotspur. The chief supporter of Henry IV in his usurpation of the throne, Northumberland feels that Henry has not heaped the honors on him that he deserves. His illness (perhaps feigned: cf. *II Henry IV*, Induction, II, 36-37) prevents him from coming to the aid of Hotspur at Shrewsbury.

HENRY PERCY, surnamed Hotspur. Although Hotspur was historically older than Henry IV, Shakespeare has reduced his age to use him as a foil for Hal (Hal, historically, was only sixteen at the time of Shrewsbury). Hotspur has all the chivalric virtues, but he is an anomaly at the centralized court of Henry IV. Noble as he is, to Shakespeare's audience as to us, he is in reality a "valiant rebel." His unrealistic plan (III, i) to divide the kingdom shows that he has little common sense, and the bickering that goes on over the division alienates our sympathies from him. A divided kingdom can mean only constant civil war.

SIR JOHN FALSTAFF, Shakespeare's supreme triumph of comic characterization. Often called the greatest comic character in the world's literature, Falstaff, through cowardice, gluttony, and drunkenness, can get into constant scrapes, but like a cat can land immediately on his feet. His bibulous humor and infectious conversation have endeared him to audiences to this day. Undoubtedly Shakespeare meant to portray him as a misleader of Hal; but the character got away from him. Although Falstaff was originally called Sir John Oldcastle (cf. I, ii, 47-48), Shakespeare was forced to change the name because of the objections of a descendant of the real Oldcastle.

## *Supporting Characters*

ARCHIBALD, Earl of Douglas, a rebel

SIR WALTER BLUNT, of the King's party, killed at Shrewsbury

OWEN GLENDOWER, Welshman, father-in-law to Mortimer, and a rebel

PRINCE JOHN OF LANCASTER, younger brother to Hal

SIR MICHAEL, a friend to the Archbishop of York

EDMUND MORTIMER, Earl of March, a rebel. See King Henry IV above

LADY MORTIMER, wife of Mortimer

LADY PERCY, wife to Hotspur and sister to Mortimer

POINS; GADSHILL; PETO; BARDOLPH, of Falstaff's group of rogues

MISTRESS QUICKLY, hostess of the Boar's-Head Tavern

RICHARD SCROOP, Archbishop of York, a rebel

SIR RICHARD VERNON, Worcester's right-hand man

EARL OF WESTMORELAND, Henry IV's general

(Lords; Officers; Sheriff; Vintner; Chamberlain; Drawers; two Carriers; Travelers; and Attendants)

(Place: *England and Wales*)

BACKGROUND. Probably composed in 1597, the play was entered in the Stationers' Register early in 1598. There are seven quartos: 1598, 1599, 1603, 1604, 1608, 1613, and 1622. The First Folio version follows the fifth quarto. The source is Holinshed's *Chronicle*.

## ACT BY ACT ANALYSIS

**ACT I.** Because of rebellions on various frontiers of the kingdom, Henry IV is unable to go on his crusade to expiate the death of Richard II: (1) Edmund Mortimer, carrying the King's colors against the Welshman Owen Glendower, has been defeated and captured; (2) Hotspur, fighting for the King, has defeated the Scotch Earl of Douglas and taken many prisoners. The King, hearing of Hotspur's prowess, bewails the dissipation of his son Prince Hal and is almost ready to wish that his boy were a changeling (**i**). When Hotspur comes to court, Henry demands the Scotch prisoners, for on the battlefield Hotspur has refused to give them up to the King's messenger. Hotspur again flatly refuses to yield them unless Henry pay ransom for Mortimer, Hotspur's brother-in-law. The King is reluctant to aid Mortimer, for he has heard that Mortimer has allied himself with Glendower and has married the Welshman's daughter. When the King delivers an ultimatum and leaves the room, Hotspur, sputtering with anger, denounces Henry. His uncle, Worcester, and his father, Northumberland, finally calm him by promising to foment a rebellion against Henry. They intend to ally their forces with those of the Archbishop of York, Glendower, Mortimer, and Douglas (**iii**). Meanwhile, Poins and Prince Hal have a plan to discomfort Falstaff. Falstaff, with others of his band of roisterers, intends to hide at Gadshill and to rob pilgrims going to Canterbury and traders traveling to London. Poins and Hal, pretending to fall in with the plan, intend to disguise themselves and rob the robbers. Then Hal in a soliloquy affirms his intention to reform when the time is ripe (**ii**).

**ACT II.** Poins and Hal hide themselves and attack Falstaff and his company after they have robbed some travelers. Falstaff runs away, leaving the booty behind him (**ii**). When the group returns to the Boar's-Head tavern, Falstaff tells a gradually growing tall tale about the thieves who have attacked him. The

Prince and Poins reveal that they were the second robbers, but Falstaff, always able to land on his feet, wriggles out of his predicament. After word comes of the Percy rebellion, an amusing scene follows in which Falstaff plays first King Henry and then Prince Hal, while the Prince, in turn, plays himself and his father (**iv**).

**ACT III.** The Percies, Mortimer, and Glendower meet to parcel out the yet-unwon kingdom. After considerable bickering, they decide that Glendower shall rule the west, the Percies the north, and Mortimer the south (**i**). At the palace the King chides Hal for his behavior, even intimating that Hal could easily become a traitor. The Prince simply and nobly answers his father that he will hereafter be more himself and will redeem his misdeeds on Percy's head (**ii**). Ready to depart for the war, Hal pays another visit to his companions at the tavern. There he discovers Falstaff in an argument with the hostess over money. After teasing Falstaff for a time, he gives command of a foot company to the fat knight (**iii**).

**ACT IV.** At the rebel camp near Shrewsbury, Hotspur learns that he will have to fight without his father, who is ill, and without Glendower, who for some reason is unable to "draw his power this fourteen days." Undiscouraged, Hotspur feels that the fewer men, the more glory (**i**). Meanwhile, Falstaff, who has been misusing the King's press by allowing the good recruits to buy their way out, meets Hal and joins forces with him (**ii**). Into the rebel camp nearby comes Sir Walter Blunt as an emissary from the King. After a long harangue by Hotspur, telling of the grievances of the rebels, the Percies agree that Worcester may attend a parley with the King (**iii**).

**ACT V.** At the parley the King offers fair terms to the rebels, and Hal offers to settle the dispute in single combat with Hotspur (**i**). However, Worcester and Vernon, the rebel emissaries, decide to conceal these peace offers. Worcester is sure that Hotspur, since he is a young man, may eventually be forgiven, but that the older heads in the conspiracy must of necessity suffer from the King's displeasure. Consequently, when the two bring back to Hotspur a report that the King will grant no mercy, the battle must be fought (**ii**). As the battle rages, the

Earl of Douglas kills both Lord Stafford and Blunt, who are dressed in the King's clothing. Falstaff, avoiding any direct combat, carries a bottle of sack instead of a pistol, to the great disgust of Hal (iii). When the real King is menaced by Douglas, Hal enters the combat and forces Douglas to flee. Finally, in simultaneous combat, Hal kills Hotspur, and Douglas forces Falstaff to simulate death to avoid being killed (iv). The battle over, the King orders Worcester and Vernon to execution, but Hal frees Douglas. The King's party will now divide: Lord John of Lancaster and Westmoreland will go to fight Northumberland and the Archbishop of York; Hal and his father will hasten to Wales to dispose of Glendower and Mortimer (v).

# THE SECOND PART OF HENRY THE FOURTH

## Cast of Characters
### *Main Characters*

KING HENRY IV. Still the same realistic Bolingbroke, the King is noticeably older and weaker in this play, aged primarily by worry and sleeplessness.

HENRY, PRINCE OF WALES, afterwards crowned Henry V. Hal in this play grows from an irresponsible youth to an early maturity which augurs well for the Kingdom. Although this play is loaded with comic scenes, Shakespeare is careful to introduce Hal into only one of them. Hal does not meet Falstaff from Act II to Act V, when he casts off the old knight; and he is associated with none of Falstaff's roistering or misdemeanors. Interestingly, too, Shakespeare makes Prince John rather than Hal deal treacherously with the rebels.

SIR JOHN FALSTAFF. Falstaff in this play undergoes a certain degeneration. Undoubtedly, Shakespeare had a bear by the tail after the success of *I Henry IV;* people came to the theater primarily to see Falstaff. However, it would be unthinkable to keep Falstaff at the court of Henry V, whom Shakespeare conceived as the greatest of the medieval kings; consequently, Shakespeare allows us to see Falstaff misuse the King's press (only mentioned in *I Henry IV*), to follow him into his relationships with harlots, and to watch him gull Shallow and Silence. In spite of this degeneration, the fat knight retains the faculty of lighting on his feet in each tight spot—until the last scene, in which he is utterly crushed.

### *Supporting Characters*

Rebels: LORD BARDOLPH; LORD HASTINGS; MORTON and TRAVERS, retainers of Northumberland; LORD MOWBRAY, son of the Mowbray in *Richard II*, who opposed Bolingbroke; EARL OF NORTHUMBERLAND, whose cowardice ruins the rebels; RICHARD SCROOP, Archbishop of York; SIR JOHN COLVILLE

Friends and Retainers of Falstaff: BARDOLPH; Falstaff's PAGE; PISTOL; PETO; POINS

The King's Party: GOWER; HARCOURT; LORD CHIEF-JUSTICE, who has arrested Hal in one of his early escapades; EARL OF SURREY; EARL OF WARWICK; EARL OF WESTMORELAND; BLUNT

Sons of Henry IV (and brothers of Henry V): PRINCE HUMPHREY OF GLOUCESTER; PRINCE JOHN OF LANCASTER, Falstaff characterizes him as devoid of humor (he tricks the Archbishop of York into dispersing his army); THOMAS, DUKE OF CLARENCE

Northumberland's WIFE and LADY PERCY, who persuade Northumberland to seek safety in Scotland

QUICKLY, hostess of a tavern in Eastcheap

RUMOUR, the Presenter

SHALLOW and SILENCE, country justices and gulls of Falstaff

DOLL TEARSHEET, Falstaff's drab

(MOULDY; SHADOW; WART; FEEBLE; BULLCALF, country soldiers; DAVY, servant of Shallow; FANG and SNARE, two Sergeants who try to arrest Falstaff; Lords and Attendants; Porters; Drawers; Beadles; Grooms; Servants; a Dancer as EPILOGUE)

(Place: *England*)

BACKGROUND. The date of composition is probably 1597; the only quarto was published in 1600. Modern texts are based on both the quarto and the First Folio (1623). The principal source is Holinshed's *Chronicle*. Shakespeare may have received hints from either Elyot's *Governour* (1531) or Stow's *Annals*.

## ACT BY ACT ANALYSIS

ACT I. The Earl of Northumberland anxiously awaits news from the battle at Shrewsbury, where his son Hotspur has opposed the army of Henry IV. At first the rumors are favorable, but eventually he hears the whole sad story: Hotspur has been killed by Prince Hal; Worcester and Douglas have both been taken prisoner. Northumberland, who, supposedly, has been ill during the battle, determines to join his army to that of the Archbishop of York in order to oppose the King's army which is marching to the North under the leadership of Westmoreland and Prince John (i). Meanwhile, the Archbishop, who is a religious as well as a temporal leader, consults with Hastings, Mowbray, and Lord Bardolph, and decides to wait for Northumberland to come up before he attempts to meet the King's army. He, together with his family, has been a consistent supporter of the dead king, Richard II, and considers Henry an usurper (iii). In London, Falstaff meets with the Chief-Justice, who chides him as a lawbreaker and an evil counselor to young Prince Hal. Falstaff, as usual, has an answer; and being short of money, he decides to borrow from any and all of his friends before he leaves on the expedition against Northumberland (ii).

**ACT II.** Falstaff is arrested by Sergeants at the suit of Mistress Quickly, to whom the fat knight owes a considerable sum. He tries to bluster his way out; but he is in real trouble when the Chief-Justice appears on the scene, and he is saved only by a call to return to his company (i). Hal, who has returned from Wales with his father, has one last fling with his companions. Hal realizes that if he mourns too obviously for his ailing father, people will take him for a hypocrite. Together with Poins, he decides to disguise himself as a waiter and to observe Falstaff with his drab, Doll Tearsheet (ii). After Falstaff makes derogatory remarks about Hal and Poins, they reveal themselves. The fat knight, as usual, lands on his feet. Then when word comes that Falstaff is wanted by the army, Hal, suddenly struck with remorse, determines to hasten back to his father, saying significantly in parting, "Falstaff, good night." (iv). Meanwhile, the cowardly Northumberland is rather easily persuaded by his wife and daughter-in-law to desert the Archbishop and to seek safety in Scotland. There he will await the outcome of the battle between the Archbishop and Westmoreland before committing himself (iii).

**ACT III.** In London the King, ill and tired, soliloquizes on the sleeplessness and worry involved in the kingship. He obtains some measure of cheer, however, from word that Glendower is dead (i). Falstaff, on his way to battle, begins to "press" men for his company. In Gloucestershire at the home of an old acquaintance, Justice Shallow, Falstaff dismisses the recruits who can pay and presses an ill-assorted lot who cannot afford to buy their way out. Falstaff intends to return to Shallow's home after the war and to milk the Justice for all the money he can get from him (ii).

**ACT IV.** In Yorkshire when the rebels hear of the defection of Northumberland, all of them but Mowbray are overjoyed to hear Westmoreland suggest a parley (**i**); but when the rebels disperse their army according to the agreement reached at the parley, Lancaster treacherously orders the Archbishop, Mowbray, and Hastings to execution. He justifies his action on the premise that nothing is due to rebels (**ii**). Falstaff, who has arrived too late to fight, captures a fleeing rebel and receives a halfhearted commendation from the leaders of the army (**iii**). Meanwhile, at London, the King is stricken with apoplexy on hearing the good news that Northumberland and Lord Bardolph have been defeated. Before the stroke he has suggested to his son Clarence, Hal's favorite brother, that he stand between Hal's other brothers and Hal's irresponsibility when the old King is dead (**iv**). The group now carries the King into another chamber, where Hal finds him. The Prince curses the crown lying on his sleeping father's bed as being responsible for his father's illness, and carries it out with him. The King, who awakens and misses the crown, suspects that Hal wishes for his early death. When Hal returns with the crown, Henry accuses him of premature assumption of the kingship. Hal tearfully explains to his father what he has done and receives the King's dying instructions, which include suggestions that foreign wars may unite the kingdom and that the people who have resented Henry IV as a usurper will not resent his son as king. The King is carried to the Jerusalem chamber to die; thus the prophecy that he will die in Jerusalem is fulfilled, although Henry has always assumed that it meant that he would go on a crusade (**v**).

**ACT V.** After the King has died, Henry V comes out to his brothers and tells them that he will be brother and father to them. He informs the Chief-Justice, who in the past has arrested him in one of his escapades, that the Justice is to chastise any of Hal's erring sons as he has chastised Hal (**ii**). Meanwhile, in Gloucestershire, Falstaff hears of the King's death and hastens to London to claim a place of honor from Hal (**iii**). At the coronation, however, Hal casts his old friend aside and orders him to reform before he will grant Falstaff any more than a pittance. King Henry V now intends to call his Parliament together to consider resuming the wars with France (**v**).

# THE LIFE OF HENRY THE FIFTH

## Cast of Characters

### Main Characters

KING HENRY V. Prince Hal has grown to maturity and is now "the mirror of all Christian kings." Shakespeare has traced the development of the young monarch from youthful irresponsibility in *I Henry IV*, through a gradual growth in seriousness in *II Henry IV*, to fulfillment in *Henry V*. However, Hal never loses his sense of humor or his love for a practical joke. Even at Agincourt the King gives his humor full play. He is his father's son and a realistic politician, but he is always more than a mere realist.

FLUELLEN, a Welsh Captain. Although it was common in Elizabethan England to make fun of the Welsh, Shakespeare presents Fluellen as a valiant warrior, serious and dogmatic to be sure, but a tower of strength to the English.

PISTOL. As the successor to Falstaff, Pistol suffers by comparison with the fat knight. However, as a rogue who rants misquoted speeches from plays and who seems as brave as a lion, Pistol, through his cowardice, adds moments of comedy to the play.

KATHARINE, daughter of the French King. Katharine has evidently fallen in love with Henry before she meets him. She seems to have sufficient spirit to cope with the ebullient young King.

### Supporting Characters

Soldiers in the English Army: BARDOLPH; NYM; BOY, page of Pistol, Nym, and Bardolph; BATES; COURT; WILLIAMS

Brothers of King Henry: DUKE OF BEDFORD; DUKE OF GLOUCESTER;

Conspirators, executed by King Henry: EARL OF CAMBRIDGE, younger brother of the Duke of York; SIR THOMAS GREY; and LORD SCROOP, an early companion of Henry

Churchmen, who expound the Salique Law: ARCHBISHOP OF
    CANTERBURY; and BISHOP OF ELY

CHORUS, who speaks the Prologues and Epilogues. Shakespeare
    rarely used prologues, but here the nature of his material and
    the moves across the Channel require the use of the Chorus.

DUKE OF EXETER, uncle of Henry

Officers in Henry's army: GOWER; JAMY, a Scotch Captain;
    MACMORRIS, an Irish Captain; SIR THOMAS ERPINGHAM

HOSTESS of a tavern in Eastcheap, formerly Mistress Quickly, now
    married to Pistol

English military leaders: EARL OF SALISBURY; EARL OF WARWICK;
    and EARL OF WESTMORELAND

DUKE OF YORK, Henry's cousin. He is the Aumerle of *Richard II*.

The French: ALICE, Katharine's lady and her tutor in English;
    DUKES OF BURGUNDY, BOURBON, and ORLEANS, leaders of the
    army; CHARLES VI, King of France; ISABEL, Queen of France;
    LEWIS, the Dauphin, a flamboyant egoist; MONTJOY, a Herald;
    RAMBURES and GRANDPRÉ, French Lords; Constable of France.

(GOVERNOR of Harfleur; French Ambassadors to the King
of England; a Herald; Lords; Ladies; Officers; Soldiers;
Citizens; Messengers and Attendants)

(Place: *England; France*)

BACKGROUND. Written in 1599, this play was published in a quarto
in 1600. This is a mangled quarto, and the text in the First Folio
(1623) is the accepted one. The principal source is Holinshed's
*Chronicle;* but Shakespeare undoubtedly made use of an earlier play
*The Famous Victories of Henry the Fifth.*

## ACT BY ACT ANALYSIS

ACT I. Henry V, contemplating renewing the wars with France,
has requested the Archbishop of Canterbury to enlighten him
concerning the rights and claims of the English King in France
(i). The Archbishop informs him that the Salique Law, which
the French have invoked to keep Henry from the overlordship
of France, has no bearing on his claims. This law is based on
the proposition that in Salique land no woman can succeed to
the throne; however, the Archbishop points out that (1) Salique
land is not in France but in Germany; (2) the French King's
claim to the throne itself descends from a woman. When Henry
has decided that his cause is just, he calls in the French ambas-

sadors, who present him with tennis balls in lieu of other tribute
—an insult which has reference to Henry's earlier giddy life (ii).

**ACT II.** Bardolph, Nym, and Pistol, preparing to leave with
the army for France, hear that Falstaff lies mortally ill. The
Hostess, whom Pistol has married, requests them to come to
the old knight's bedside (i). Falstaff dies babbling "of green
fields," and the "irregulars" leave to join the army (iii). Meanwhile, Henry has discovered that the Earl of Cambridge, Lord
Scroop, and Sir Thomas Grey have been paid by France to
murder him. The King traps them into confessions and orders
their execution, not because of their treachery to him personally,
but because of their tampering with the safety of the Kingdom
(ii). In France, Exeter arrives at court with the pedigree which
supports Henry's claim to the French throne. The French King
offers to consider the matter and to return an answer upon
the morrow (iv).

**ACT III.** The French King's counteroffer being insufficient
(Prologue), the English land in France and besiege Harfleur (i).
Henry has obviously united the British Isles behind him, for at
the siege of Harfleur are Fluellen, a Welsh Captain; Macmorris,
an Irish Captain; and Jamy, a Scotch Captain. The three are
arguing, when a parley is sounded (ii). At the parley, the Governor of Harfleur, unable to obtain reinforcements, yields the
city to the English (iii). When the English establish camp in
Picardy, Pistol gets embroiled with Fluellen over the fate of
Bardolph, who has "stolen a pax" and must be hanged. Fluellen
refuses to intercede in the affair and receives the King's commendation: there must be no looting. When Montjoy, the
French herald, arrives with the French suggestion that Henry
"consider of his ransom," Henry replies that although his army
is sick and reduced in number, the English will neither look for
nor avoid a battle (vi). Near Agincourt the confident French
await battle with the sadly outnumbered English (vii). Meanwhile, Katharine of France, already half in love with Henry,
attempts to learn English from an old gentlewoman (iv).

**ACT IV.** On the night before the battle, Henry walks in-
cognito around the English camp. When Michael Williams, a
soldier, takes exception to a remark of Henry's, the two exchange

gloves as gages and promise to continue the quarrel after the battle. In the course of the conversation, Williams remarks that it is not for the common soldiers to worry about the righteousness of a war. They must obey the King, and their sins are on his head if the quarrel be unjust. Struck with this thought, Henry realizes the great responsibilities of a ruler and prays that his father's sin in deposing Richard II be not visited on the English in this battle (i). In the morning the French prepare confidently for the battle (ii). In the English camp Henry scoffs at the idea that the English could use reinforcements: the honor will be the greater because of the odds against them. When Montjoy again appears and suggests that Henry ransom himself, the King throws the taunt back in his face (iii). The English thereupon soundly defeat the first charge of the French (v), but the French rally and attack the English luggage and the boys guarding it. Henry orders the English to kill their prisoners and to throw back the French (vi). Montjoy enters again to admit that the English have won the day. Henry, yielding to a prankish impulse, gives Williams' glove to Fluellen, telling him that the glove is Alencon's and that if any man challenge it, he is a traitor (vii). When Williams strikes Fluellen, the Welshman arrests him and takes him to the King. Henry admits that he has been the challenger and fills Williams' glove with money. He then receives the unbelievable news that in the battle some ten thousand French have been slain to less than thirty English (viii).

**ACT V.** Henry returns in triumph to England and then goes back to France (Prologue). When Pistol has foolishly twitted Fluellen about his leek on St. Davy's Day, the Welshman strikes him and forces him to eat the leek. Since Bardolph and Nym have both been hanged for theft (IV, iv), Pistol determines to return to England and trade on the scars given him by Fluellen, by pretending to have received them in battle (i). Thoroughly defeated, the French King accedes to Henry's demands and gives him Katharine in marriage. Henry's forward wooing of Katharine affrights but pleases her. Everyone hopes that this marriage will unite the two kingdoms in amity (ii). However, the Chorus is full of forebodings of Henry's early death and his son's loss of all of Henry's gains (Epilogue).

# THE FIRST PART OF
# HENRY THE SIXTH

## Cast of Characters

### *Main Characters*

KING HENRY VI. Since Henry VI was less than a year old when his father died, his minority was plagued by a jockeying for power among his relatives and other nobles. Never a strong king, Henry is depicted by Shakespeare as a physical coward devoted primarily to his religion.

DUKE OF GLOUCESTER, uncle of the King, and Protector. Shakespeare consistently characterized this younger bother of Henry V as a good and honest man beset by so much contention that he is unable to rule well. This play is concerned in considerable part with the running feud between Gloucester and his uncle the Bishop of Winchester.

HENRY BEAUFORT, Bishop of Winchester (afterwards Cardinal), great-uncle to the King. As the chief antagonist to Gloucester, this churchman constantly strives to overthrow the Protectorate and to supersede Gloucester.

JOHN BEAUFORT, Earl of Somerset, afterwards made Duke, nephew of Henry Beaufort. Besides the quarrel over the Protectorship, Shakespeare introduces into this play the beginning of the quarrels leading to the Wars of the Roses. Somerset is here the chief spokesman for the Lancastrian, or Red-rose, faction.

RICHARD PLANTAGENET, son of Richard, late Earl of Cambridge, afterwards Duke of York. When Richard discovers that his claim to the throne is better than Henry's, he begins the machinations which afterwards lead to the overthrow of the Lancastrians—this even though Henry restores his title, forefeited by his father's treason to Henry V. Richard's claim to the throne descends from his mother, whose great-grandfather was the third son of Edward III. On his father's side he is descended from Edmond, Duke of York, the fifth son of Edward III. He becomes the focal point for the Yorkist, or White-rose, faction.

EARL OF WARWICK. Although he plays a small part in this play, he becomes constantly more important as the series proceeds: eventually he is called the "King maker."

EARL OF SUFFOLK. He falls in love with Margaret and arranges her marriage to Henry, in spite of the objections of Gloucester.

LORD TALBOT, afterwards Earl of Shrewsbury, the great leader of the English forces in France. He is killed at Bordeaux.

MARGARET, daughter of Reignier, afterwards married to Henry VI. Margaret allows her paramour Suffolk to arrange the marriage to Henry. She later becomes a moving force in English politics.

JOAN LA PUCELLE, commonly called Joan of Arc. Shakespeare, not unnaturally, depicts her as in league with devils rather than with the forces of good.

### Supporting Characters

DUKE OF ALENCON, of the French royal family

BASSET, of the Red-rose faction

DUKE OF BEDFORD, uncle to the King, and Regent of France

THOMAS BEAUFORT, Duke of Exeter and great-uncle of the King

DUKE OF BURGUNDY, originally of the English faction in France, afterward, under the influence of la Pucelle, shifting to the French

BASTARD OF ORLEANS, a member of-the French royal family

CHARLES, Dauphin, afterwards King of France

SIR JOHN FASTOLFE. His precipitant retreats more than once defeat the English in France

A LAWYER

SIR WILLIAM LUCY, SIR WILLIAM GLANSDALE, SIR THOMAS GAR-GRAVE, with the English armies in France

MAYOR OF LONDON, the voice of the people of London

EDMUND MORTIMER, Earl of March, uncle to Richard Plantagenet. Before Mortimer dies, he whets Richard's appetite for the kingship

MORTIMER'S KEEPERS

REIGNIER, Duke of Anjou, and titular King of Naples, father of Margaret

EARL OF SALISBURY, killed by the French at Orleans

JOHN TALBOT, son to Lord Talbot, killed with his father

VERNON, of the White Rose faction

WOODVILLE, lieutenant of the Tower

(Governor of Paris; Master-Gunner of Orleans and his Son; General of the French forces in Bordeaux; a French Sergeant; a Porter; an old Shepherd, father to Joan la Pucelle; COUNTESS OF AUVERGNE, fomenter of an abortive plot against Talbot; Lords; Wardens of the Tower; Officers; Messengers; Heralds; Soldiers; and Attendants, English and French; Fiends appearing to la Pucelle)

(Place: *Partly in England, and partly in France.*)

BACKGROUND. This play was first published in the First Folio (1623). The composition date is probably 1591. The sources are the *Chronicles* of Holinshed and Halle.

## ACT BY ACT ANALYSIS

ACT I. The great monarch Henry V has just died, leaving a nine-month-old son. The kingdom, consequently, is a protectorate under the rule of the Duke of Gloucester, younger brother of Henry V. However, the Bishop of Winchester, uncle to Gloucester, is ambitious to usurp the Protectorship, and the Court is full of recriminations between the Bishop and Gloucester. Because of these broils, the French to a considerable extent have recouped their losses sustained at the hands of Henry V. The Duke of Bedford, Gloucester's brother and Regent of France, is forced to leave England hurriedly. His mission is an attempt to retrieve the disasters in France; for the Dauphin has been crowned at Rheims, and Talbot, the great English general, has been taken prisoner (i). Meanwhile the feud between Gloucester and Winchester has spread to their servants, and rioting takes place before the Tower (iii). In France, Joan la Pucelle, a maiden, comes to Charles, the Dauphin, and tells him that she is destined to lead the French forces to victory. He, half doubtful at first, accepts her offer of aid (ii). Before Orleans the English have the misfortune to lose Salisbury and Gargrave, both killed by a gun from the town (iv). Joan, now leading the French, drives the English from Orleans after a single combat between her and Talbot, in which neither can prevail (v).

**ACT II.** Talbot, Burgundy, and Bedford attack by stealth the French in Orleans and drive them from the city (**i**). While Talbot is occupying Orleans, he receives an invitation to visit the Countess of Auvergne (**ii**). Not quite trusting the Countess, who in reality intends to trap and kill him, Talbot carefully posts men outside her castle. When she attempts to take him prisoner, he calls the men; and she is tremendously impressed by his qualities of leadership (**iii**). Meanwhile, in London there is a disagreement between Somerset of the Lancastrian faction and Richard Plantagenet of the Yorkist group. The men around them choose sides in the quarrel and pluck red and white roses as symbols of their choices: thus the Wars of the Roses are foreshadowed (**iv**). Before Edmund Mortimer dies in the Tower, he calls his nephew Richard Plantagenet to him and explains: first, that Richard, being descended from Lionel, has a better claim to the throne than the reigning Lancastrians, who are descended from John of Gaunt; and secondly, that since Richard Cambridge, Richard's father, was unrightfully accused of treason to Henry V, Richard has thereby been deprived unjustly of his estates and title as Duke of York. Richard determines to play for the throne (**v**).

**ACT III.** When Richard hastens to court to claim his estates, he finds young Henry VI himself attempting to make peace between Gloucester and Winchester after a broil between their servants has upset the London streets. The King achieves, at best, an uneasy truce. Before Henry leaves for Paris to be crowned, he restores, at the request of Warwick, Richard Plantagenet's estates and title as Duke of York (**i**). Meanwhile, the French, by a ruse, drive the English from Rouen and, in turn, are driven from the city by Talbot (**ii**). As the French retire from Rouen, la Pucelle meets Burgundy, and, appealing to his patriotism, induces him to desert the English and fight for France (**iii**).

**ACT IV.** At Henry's coronation the feud between the Lancastrians and Yorkists breaks out anew. The young King, as a Lancastrian, puts on a red rose, but insists that he loves both branches of the family and declares that all Englishmen must unite to defeat the French. He appoints York as the Regent of France and Somerset as second in command (**i**). When Talbot is surrounded by the French at Bordeaux, York blames Somerset for not relieving him (**iii**), and Somerset in turn throws all the blame on York (**iv**). Talbot's young son John has come to fight by the side of his father, and he refuses to save his life by flying to safety (**v, vi**). Both Talbot and John are slain by the French (**vii**).

**ACT V.** Gloucester suggests to Henry that he accept the offers of the Pope, the Emperor, and the Earl of Armagnac to mediate the strife between England and France and, to insure lasting peace, that he marry the daughter of the Earl of Armagnac, a relative of Charles the Dauphin. Meanwhile, Winchester, who has paid heavily for a Cardinal's hat, is made ambassador to seal the peace (**i**). The English now prepare to attack the French (**ii**). Before Angiers, Pucelle's "fiends" desert her, and she is captured by York (**iii**); however, before she is executed, she, in order to maintain her prestige as divinely inspired, denies her old father, a poor shepherd. In spite of her terror, which leads her to claim that she is with child, she is burnt at the stake (**iv**). The Duke of Suffolk captures Margaret, daughter of Reignier, falls in love with her, and determines to make her Henry's Queen so that, since he is already married, he can enjoy her himself (**iii**). In spite of York's secret chagrin at the loss of part of his (he hopes) future kingdom, peace is made between France and England. Charles agrees to swear allegiance to Henry and to remain in France as Henry's Viceroy; the English agree to maintain no interest in any of the French towns of garrison (**iv**). Against the advice of Gloucester, Henry, now in London, falls in love with Suffolk's word picture of Margaret and determines to make her his Queen in spite of the fact that she has no dower. Suffolk now is positive that he can rule the realm through Margaret (**v**).

# THE SECOND PART OF HENRY THE SIXTH

## Cast of Characters

### *Main Characters*

KING HENRY VI, last of the Lancastrian Kings. The King in this play spends increasingly more time at devotions and less at affairs of state. His Queen constantly assumes more power and eventually leads the army against Richard Plantagenet, the Yorkist pretender.

HUMPHREY, Duke of Gloucester, Henry's uncle. Gloucester as Lord Protector falls victim to the machinations of Winchester, Suffolk, and Margaret. His death helps to precipitate a crisis for the Lancastrians.

CARDINAL BEAUFORT, Bishop of Winchester, and deadly enemy of Gloucester. He rids himself of Gloucester but soon dies of a mysterious ailment.

RICHARD PLANTAGENET, Duke of York. Richard allows events (with some pushing on his part) to further his ambitions to supersede Henry as King. He foments the Jack Cade rebellion to weaken the kingdom; and upon his return from Ireland he easily defeats the Lancastrians.

EDWARD and RICHARD, his sons. Richard especially is an effective leader for his father's forces. We see him here as a blunt, but vigorous warrior. In this play there is no foreshadowing of his later devilishness as Richard III.

DUKE OF SUFFOLK, the Queen's paramour. The murder of Gloucester on Suffolk's order causes his downfall and death.

EARL OF WARWICK, the king maker. He is the military right arm of Richard Plantagenet.

JACK CADE, a rebel. He leads a rebellion of the common people in Kent. When this movement spreads to London, even the King and Queen are forced to flee.

MARGARET, Queen to King Henry. Shakespeare characterizes her as much more masterful and masculine than her husband. Throughout the play she consistently rules him and finally leads his army against Richard.

ELEANOR, Duchess of Gloucester. Her relations with conjurers lead to her disgrace and eventually to her husband's downfall and death.

## Supporting Characters

ROGER BOLINGBROKE, the conjurer

DUKE OF BUCKINGHAM, a supporter of Henry

DUKE OF SOMERSET, a supporter of Henry

LORD CLIFFORD, a military leader for Henry

YOUNG CLIFFORD, his son, who, when he sees his father dead, vows revenge on the House of York

TWO GENTLEMEN, prisoners with Suffolk

MATTHEW GOFFE, killed in the Cade rebellion

THOMAS HORNER, an armorer, and PETER, his man. When Peter accuses his master of treason, the two fight a duel before the court

JOHN HUME and JOHN SOUTHWELL, priests who arrange conjuring tricks for Eleanor

ALEXANDER IDEN, a Kentish gentleman who captures Cade

A LIEUTENANT, MASTER, MASTER'S MATE, WALTER WHITMORE, and other pirates, captors and executioners of Suffolk

EARL OF SALISBURY, father of Warwick and a Yorkist partisan

LORD SAY, a courtier and favorite of Margaret

LORD SCALES, in charge of the Tower

SIR HUMPHREY STAFFORD and WILLIAM STAFFORD, his brother, both killed in Kent in the early days of the Cade rebellion

SIR JOHN STANLEY, the guard who leads Eleanor to exile

VAUX, a messenger at court

(CLERK of Chatham; MAYOR of St. Alban's; SIMPCOX, an imposter; GEORGE BEVIS, JOHN HOLLAND, DICK the butcher, SMITH the weaver, MICHAEL, etc., followers of Cade; two MURDERERS; MARGERY JORDAIN, a witch; WIFE of Simpcox; a Spirit; Lords, Ladies, Attendants; Petitioners; Aldermen; a Herald; a Beadle, Sheriff, and Officers; Citizens; Apprentices; Falconers; Guards; Soldiers; Messengers, etc.)

(Place:  *England*)

BACKGROUND. Probably composed in 1591, this play appeared, to-
gether with parts of *III Henry VI,* in a pirated quarto in 1595. The
First Folio (1623) has a much longer text. The sources are the
*Chronicles* of Holinshed and Halle.

## ACT BY ACT ANALYSIS

**ACT I.** The Duke of Suffolk has returned from France with
Margaret of Anjou as a bride for Henry VI; her father, Reignier,
not only has refused Henry a dowry for his daughter but also,
knowing that Henry desires Margaret, he has demanded that
the English return his French possessions to him. The King,
pleased with his bride, creates Suffolk a duke. When Gloucester,
the Protector, delivers a denunciation of the alliance, his enemy
Cardinal Beaufort perceives an opportunity to disgrace him.
Beaufort intends to side with the Queen and Suffolk in their
endeavors to rule the country. The Duke of York, on the other
hand, decides to play off one faction against the other in order
to further his own ambition to mount the throne (**i**). Meanwhile,
the Duchess of Gloucester, in direct violation of the law, has
been listening to witches and conjurers furnished her by Hume,
who is in the pay of Suffolk and the Cardinal (**ii**). While the
conjuring proceeds, the Dukes of Buckingham and York break
in on the seance and take prisoner the Duchess and the
magicians. The Dukes discover in a paper cryptic prophecies
that "the duke yet lives that Henry shall depose; but him outlive
and die a violent death"; that Suffolk shall die by water; and that
Somerset must shun castles (**iv**). At the palace the Queen and
Suffolk study means to be rid of Gloucester. When Gloucester
supports York for Regent of France, Suffolk and the Queen
demand instead that Somerset be appointed. Gloucester is so
angered by their accusations that he must leave the room, to
compose himself. By the time he returns, a quarrel between
Horner and his man Peter has come to the attention of the
court. Peter accuses his master of having said that the Duke of
York is the rightful heir to the crown; consequently, because
of a possible suspicion against York, Gloucester consents to
the appointment of Somerset as Regent. Horner and Peter are
ordered to fight in single combat to settle the dispute between
them (**iii**).

**ACT II.** At court Gloucester and the Cardinal make an appointment for a duel; but when Buckingham enters with news that the Duchess has been apprehended in a seance, the duel becomes impossible (**i**). York outlines to Warwick and Salisbury his claim to the throne; the two earls decide to support him (**ii**). At the trial of the Duchess she is convicted of treason and banished to the Isle of Man. At the same time Henry relieves Gloucester of his staff of office (**iii**). Unable to condone his wife's sin, Gloucester bids her farewell. He is summoned to appear at the King's Parliament at Bury St. Edmund's (**iv**). Meanwhile Peter kills his drunken master in their combat (**iii**).

**ACT III.** At Bury St. Edmund's, Somerset reports that France is totally lost. When Suffolk accuses Gloucester of high treason, Gloucester is imprisoned, though the King hopes that he can clear himself of the charge. Because Gloucester is popular with the commons, his enemies realize that he must be killed immediately. Suffolk is appointed executioner. When news of a rebellion in Ireland reaches the court, the Cardinal, Suffolk, and the Queen, hoping to get rid of York, taunt him into accepting the leadership of the forces raised to put down the rebellion. York, seizing the opportunity to put himself at the head of an army, quickly assents to the proposal. He intends to "seduce" a Kentishman, Jack Cade of Ashford, who will assume the name of John Mortimer, heir to the crown, to raise a revolt at home. York hopes thereby to shake the throne and make it fall into his hands upon his return from Ireland (**i**). When news of the murder of Gloucester is brought to Henry, he is overcome with grief. Warwick, as representative of commons, demands Suffolk's death or banishment. In spite of the protests of the Queen, who is Suffolk's mistress, he is banished. While Suffolk and the Queen are saying farewell, word reaches them that the Cardinal is at the point of death (**ii**). The Cardinal dies in agony, trying to bribe Death for a respite (**iii**).

**ACT IV.** Suffolk is killed by Walter Whitmore, a pirate, a deed which confirms the prophecy that Suffolk would die at sea (**i**). Meanwhile in Kent the Cade rebellion is gaining adherents. The King's officers are killed by the rebels (**ii**). The Queen, grief stricken at Suffolk's death, and the King, are forced to flee before Cade, who has now reached London (**iv**). All forces sent against Cade in London are defeated (**vi, vii**). However, when Clifford and Buckingham appeal to the patriotism of Cade's army and remind them of the glory of Henry V, they turn against their leader. Cade is forced to flee (**viii**), and is killed by a Kentish gentleman, Alexander Iden (**x**). Meanwhile, the King hears that the Duke of York has returned from Ireland and is marching on London with a huge army, demanding the downfall of Somerset (**ix**).

**ACT V.** Buckingham, as an emissary from Henry, meets York and demands to know his intentions. When York dissemblingly insists that he wishes only to remove Somerset, Buckingham informs him that Somerset is already in the Tower. Meanwhile, the King has knighted Iden for killing Cade. When the King's forces meet with York, Somerset is with them. York, furious, calls his sons, Edward and Richard, and his adherents, Warwick and Salisbury, and challenges the Lancastrians to battle (**i**). In the battle of St. Alban's, Warwick kills old Clifford; Richard slays Somerset; and the King and Queen fly to London. Young Clifford swears revenge for his father's death (**ii**). The Yorkists determine to pursue the fleeing court and intend to crown York King of England (**iii**).

# THE THIRD PART OF
# HENRY THE SIXTH

## Cast of Characters

### *Main Characters*

KING HENRY VI, last of the Lancastrian Kings. In this play Henry, a physical coward, is deposed and killed by the Yorkist faction. Henry is given over entirely to his religion, leaving Margaret, Lord Clifford,˙ and others to fight his battles for him.

EDWARD, PRINCE OF WALES, his son, murdered at Tewkesbury by Richard and the Yorkists.

LORD CLIFFORD, a leader of Henry's forces. Burning with anger at the Yorkists because of his father's death at their hands, Clifford shows them no mercy. His murders of Richard Plantagenet and the young Earl of Rutland earn him the undying enmity of the Yorkists.

RICHARD PLANTAGENET, DUKE OF YORK. Richard does not reap the fruit of his rebellion. He is captured and executed by Margaret's army.

EDWARD, EARL OF MARCH, son of Richard of York, afterwards King Edward IV. He profits from his father's rebellion and the triumph of the Yorkists. His lust for women, however, earns him the enmity of Lewis XI of France: Edward, forced to marry Lady Grey to possess her, reneges on his offer of marriage to Bona, sister-in-law of Lewis.

EDMUND, EARL OF RUTLAND, young son of Richard of York, murdered by Clifford.

GEORGE, SON OF RICHARD, afterwards Duke of Clarence. Clarence, disgusted by Edward's marriage to Lady Grey, joins forces with Margaret, but afterwards, conscience stricken, he returns to the Yorkist fold.

RICHARD, afterwards Duke of Gloucester, son of Richard of York. In this play for the first time the actions of Richard fore-shadow his vicious career in *Richard III*. In Act III he states his purpose to gain the throne by fair means or foul. He it is who takes the lead in murdering Edward, Prince of Wales, and who delivers the fatal stroke to Henry VI.

EARL OF WARWICK, the king maker. Warwick is chiefly responsible for Edward's ascending the throne, but Edward humiliates him by marrying Lady Grey while Warwick is negotiating a royal marriage with Bona. Because of this humiliation, Warwick changes sides. He is later killed in battle by the Yorkists.

QUEEN MARGARET, the leading spirit of the Lancastrians. Putting on armor, she leads Henry's armies against the Yorkists.

LADY GREY, afterwards Edward IV's Queen. A widow with three children, she refuses Edward's lustful proposals. He, fascinated by her, offers her the Queenship.

## Supporting Characters

Lancastrian, or Red-rose Faction: DUKE OF EXETER; DUKE OF SOMERSET; EARL OF OXFORD; EARL OF NORTHUMBERLAND; EARL OF WESTMORELAND; HENRY, EARL OF RICHMOND, a youth, —Henry VI prophesies that Richmond will save England; SIR JOHN SOMERVILLE

Yorkist, or White-rose faction: DUKE OF NORFOLK; MARQUESS OF MONTAGUE, brother to Warwick (later shifts to Lancastrians); EARL OF PEMBROKE; LORD HASTINGS; LORD STAFFORD; SIR JOHN MORTIMER and SIR HUGH MORTIMER, uncles of the Duke of York; SIR WILLIAM STANLEY; SIR JOHN MONTGOMERY

LEWIS XI, King of France

(LORD RIVERS, brother to Lady Grey; TUTOR to Rutland; MAYOR of York; LIEUTENANT of the Tower; a Nobleman; two Keepers, who capture Henry VI; a Huntsman, who guards Edward IV as prisoner; a Son that has killed his Father; a Father that has killed his Son; BONA, sister of the French Queen; Soldiers; Attendants; Messengers; Watchmen, etc.)

### (Place: *England and France*)

BACKGROUND. This play probably was composed late in 1591 or early in 1592. Parts of *III Henry VI* appeared together with parts of *II Henry VI* in the mangled quarto of 1595. The First Folio (1623) has a longer text. The sources are the *Chronicles* of Holin-shed and Halle.

## ACT BY ACT ANALYSIS

**ACT I.** When King Henry and the Lancastrians arrive at Parliament, they find the Yorkists in control and the Duke of York sitting on the throne. York offers to give up the throne to Henry on the condition that he be made Henry's heir; Henry consents to this disinheriting of his son. When Queen Margaret arrives, however, Henry's weakness enrages her. She castigates him as a "timorous wretch," and, together with her son Prince Edward, departs to raise an army to fight York (**i**). When York hears that the Lancastrians are in the field, he, goaded by his sons Edward and Richard, gathers his forces to give them battle (**ii**). During the ensuing battle, Lord Clifford finds Rutland, York's young son, alone with his tutor, and, in spite of Rutland's noble behavior, murders the youth as revenge for his father's death (cf. *II Henry VI, V* ii) (**iii**). Queen Margaret's forces carry the day, capturing York in the course of the battle. Led by the Queen and Clifford, the Lancastrians torture the Duke, giving him a napkin stained with Rutland's blood with which to dry his eyes and putting a paper crown on his head. Finally they murder him (**iv**).

**ACT II.** Edward and Richard hear from a messenger that their father and brother are dead; whereupon they meet Warwick and Montague, who have been defeated by Margaret at St. Alban's. Edward, now pretender to the crown, asks Warwick to help him obtain his rights. The group hears that Margaret and the Lancastrians are coming to attack them (**i**). Before York, Clifford and the Queen suggest that Henry, who has less and less stomach for fighting, leave the field; for the Lancastrians have better success without him. Henry knights his son Edward, who vows to fight on for his father. The Yorkists approach for a parley, in which insults and taunts are bandied back and forth; and the battle is joined (**ii**). When the battle seems almost lost for the Yorkists, Richard rallies the Yorkists (**iii**) and defeats Clifford in personal combat (**iv**). Meanwhile, Henry, who has been watching the battle, sees a son who has killed his father and a father who has killed his son in battle. While Henry broods over his moral responsibility for such deeds, Margaret cries to him to fly; for the Yorkists are everywhere triumphant (**v**). The Yorkists survey the field and find Clifford mortally wounded. Edward makes Warwick his chief adviser and requests him to go to France to bring back Lady Bona, sister of the French Queen. Upon her arrival she will become Edward's wife and Queen of England. He then creates Richard Duke of Gloucester and George Duke of Clarence (**vi**).

**ACT III.** King Henry inadvisedly steals from exile in Scotland into the north of England, where he is recognized and captured by two keepers, who intend to turn him over to King Edward (**i**). Meanwhile, Edward, as King, has been gratifying his lust for women; but when he tries to seduce Lady Grey, a widow who has been pleading for a return of her husband's lands, she refuses his suit. Unable to obtain her by illegal means, Edward proposes to make her his Queen, though Warwick is even now in France arranging Edward's marriage to Lady Bona. Gloucester, meanwhile, intends to play for the crown by any means possible (**ii**). Warwick arrives in France to find that Margaret is already at the court of King Lewis; she has been pleading for Lewis' aid for Henry. However, Lewis inclines to favor the status quo and consents to send Lady Bona to Edward. At this moment a post arrives with letters announcing Edward's marriage to Lady Gray. Infuriated by this insult, Warwick joins forces with Margaret and the Lancastrians and betroths his daughter to young Prince Edward. Also angered by Edward's behavior, Lewis offers his aid (**iii**).

**ACT IV.** Clarence, unable to stomach his brother's marriage, deserts with Somerset to the Lancastrians. However, Richard of Gloucester, not from love of Edward but for reasons of policy, decides to remain loyal (**i**). Meanwhile, Warwick has arrived in England; and when Clarence joins him, Warwick offers his second daughter as Clarence's bride (**ii**). Near Warwick, Edward and the Yorkists meet the Duke of Warwick; the battle goes against Edward, and he is taken prisoner (**iii**). Since Warwick plans to crown Henry again, Queen Elizabeth hastens from London carrying the young prince, Edward's son (**iv**). Meanwhile, Gloucester, Hastings, and others manage to rescue Edward from Yorkshire, where he has been held prisoner (**v**). In London, meantime, Henry makes Warwick and Clarence joint protectors of England. Henry meets the young Earl of

Richmond and prophesies that he will be "England's hope."
When the court then hears that Edward has escaped and fled
to Burgundy for help in regaining his crown, Somerset and
Oxford hurry young Richmond off to Brittany, where he will
be safe from the continuing civil wars (vi). Edward, Richard,
and the Yorkists land in England, where they are joined by
Englishmen anxious to do battle with Margaret (vii). When
Warwick and Clarence leave the palace to meet Edward's
forces, Edward and Gloucester circuitously arrive at London,
capture Henry, and leave for Coventry to meet Warwick (viii).

ACT V. At Coventry, Warwick awaits the arrival of the other
Lancastrians. When Edward and his forces arrive, taunts
are thrown back and forth. Finally the other Lancastrians
arrive: Oxford, Montague, and Somerset; but when Clarence
arrives, he becomes conscience stricken, plucks the red rose
from his hat, and declares for his brothers (i). In the battle
Warwick is mortally wounded and is captured by Edward (ii).
The Yorkists, completely triumphant, plan to march to Tewks-
bury to meet Margaret and her army (iii), who there are awaiting
the Yorkists (iv). Again the Yorkists triumph; Oxford and
Somerset are beheaded; Margaret and Prince Edward are taken
prisoner. In turn, Edward, Gloucester, and Clarence stab the
young Prince. Young Edward sprawls at his mother's feet,
and she is taken out, shouting curses (v). Meanwhile, Richard
has hastened to the Tower, where he finds King Henry and
murders him, muttering after the deed is done that he intends
to do away with everyone who stands between him and the
throne (vi). In the palace Edward reigns again as King; he
meets again his Queen and his young son and hopes that the
civil broils are over. He orders Queen Margaret to exile and
feels that all his troubles have ended (vii).

# THE TRAGEDY OF RICHARD THE THIRD

## Cast of Characters

### *Main Characters*

KING EDWARD IV. The death of Edward gives Richard his opportunity to usurp the throne.

EDWARD, Prince of Wales, afterwards King Edward V, and RICHARD, Duke of York, sons to Edward. These two young Princes are smothered in the Tower on orders of Richard.

GEORGE, Duke of Clarence, brother of Edward IV. Because of his previous shifts from the Yorkist to Lancastrian and back to Yorkist factions, no one quite trusts Clarence. Richard succeeds in convincing Edward that he should order Clarence to the Tower; then Richard, by forging an order, has Clarence drowned in a malmsey butt.

RICHARD, Duke of Gloucester, afterwards King Richard III, brother to Edward IV. The villain-protagonist of the tragedy, Richard succeeds in forcibly removing all obstacles between himself and the throne. Retribution, in the person of Richmond, finally catches up with him.

HENRY, Earl of Richmond, afterwards King Henry VII. The first of the Tudor line of Kings, Henry is descended through the Beaufort line from John of Gaunt, the progenitor of the Lancastrians. His marriage to Elizabeth, daughter of Edward IV, allies him to the Yorkist faction. Thus the red and white roses are at last united.

DUKE OF BUCKINGHAM, Richard's chief ally in obtaining the throne. When Buckingham shows hesitation in approving plans for the murder of the young Princes, Richard snubs him. When Buckingham tries to join Richmond, he is captured and executed before he effects a juncture of forces.

ELIZABETH, King Edward IV's Queen. After Richard effects the deaths of her two sons, her brother, and her uncle, she supports Richmond.

MARGARET, widow of King Henry VI. Margaret curses the whole house of York and its supporters; it is this curse that the Yorkists constantly mention as, one by one, they meet violent ends.

DUCHESS OF YORK, mother of Kings Edward IV and Richard III. In spite of Richard's subtlety, the Duchess early recognizes his villainy.

LADY ANNE, widow of Edward Prince of Wales, son of Henry VI. She afterwards marries Richard. Richard's appeal to women is illustrated by his marriage to Anne, whose husband and father-in-law he has slain.

LORD HASTINGS, executed by order of Richard.

## Supporting Characters

Richard's Party: DUKE OF NORFOLK; EARL OF SURREY, Norfolk's son; SIR RICHARD RATCLIFF; SIR WILLIAM CATESBY; LORD LOVEL

Richmond's Party: LORD STANLEY, called also Earl of Derby. He must dissemble with Richard, for his son is hostage in Richard's hands; however, he throws his strength to Richmond at the psychological moment; SIR JAMES BLOUNT; CHRISTOPHER URSWICK, a Priest; SIR WALTER HERBERT; SIR WILLIAM BRANDON, Keeper in the Tower, killed at Bosworth; EARL OF OXFORD

Queen Elizabeth's Faction: MARQUIS OF DORSET and LORD GREY, Sons to Elizabeth by a former marriage (Lord Grey is executed by Richard; Dorset makes his escape to Richmond); EARL RIVERS, Brother to Elizabeth, executed by Richard; SIR THOMAS VAUGHAN, executed by Richard.

(A YOUNG SON of Clarence (Edward, Earl of Warwick), Richard considers him beneath notice, as halfwitted. CARDINAL BOURCHIER, Archbishop of Canterbury; THOMAS ROTHERHAM, Archbishop of York; JOHN MORTON, Bishop of Ely; SIR JAMES TYRREL, murderer of the little Princes; SIR ROBERT BRAKENBURY, lieutenant of the Tower, killed at Bosworth; a Priest; TRESSEL and BERKELEY, gentlemen attending on the Lady Anne; LORD MAYOR of London, who assents to Richard's coronation; SHERIFF of Wiltshire; A YOUNG DAUGHTER of Clarence (Margaret Plantagenet); Ghosts of those murdered by Richard III; Lords and other Attendants; a Pursuivant; a

Page; Scrivener; Citizens; Bishops; Aldermen; Murderers; Messengers; Soldiers; etc.)

(Place: *England*)

BACKGROUND. Probably composed about 1593, this tragedy went through seven quartos: 1597, 1602, 1605, 1612, 1622, 1629, and 1634. The version in the First Folio (1623), although far different from the ones in the quartos, is thought to be more nearly an authentic text. The sources are the *Chronicles* of Holinshed and Halle.

## ACT BY ACT ANALYSIS

**ACT I.** Richard of Gloucester, an ill-formed hunchback, has determined to reach the throne of England, no matter what the cost. Standing in his way are his eldest brother, King Edward IV, and Edward's children; and George, Duke of Clarence, and his children. His first step to rid himself of Clarence is to revive an old prophecy that "G of Edward's heirs, the murderer shall be." This prophecy he has carried to the King with insinuations that Clarence is plotting against King Edward. When Edward orders Clarence to the Tower, Richard meets him on the way and, dissembling, commiserates with him. Meanwhile, when news arrives that the King is ailing, Richard intends to marry the Lady Anne, daughter of Warwick and widow of the murdered youth Edward, Prince of Wales, the Lancastrian heir (i). Following up this plan immediately, he woos Lady Anne, who is mourning the death of her father-in-law, Henry VI (who also has been slain by Richard). Although Anne at first spurns him, Richard seems to exert a fascination over her; and, in spite of herself, she grants him her hand (ii). Meanwhile, at the palace Queen Elizabeth and her relatives Lord Rivers and Lord Grey, conscious of Richard's hatred for them, hope that when Edward dies Richard will not be appointed Protector during young Edward's minority. When Richard enters and accuses the Queen of having plotted against Clarence, bitter recriminations are thrown back and forth. At this point Queen Margaret, widow of Henry VI, enters and curses Richard, Clarence, the Queen, the Queen's children, Lord Hastings, Rivers, Dorset, and finally Buckingham. When Richard is left alone, he instructs murderers to kill Clarence in the Tower (iii). Following Richard's instructions, the first murderer stabs Clarence, who has been dreaming of death, and puts the body into a malmsey butt (iv).

**ACT II.** King Edward has just succeeded in making an uneasy peace between the Queen and her faction on the one side, and Buckingham and Hastings on the other, when Richard arrives with the news that Clarence is dead. He implies, too, that the Queen's party has tampered with Edward's messenger— the messenger who was to have reversed the order to kill Clarence (**i**). While the old Duchess of York, who already suspects Richard as the murderer, mourns the death of her son Clarence, Queen Elizabeth enters with news that King Edward is dead. Richard and Buckingham intend to accompany the group which will go to escort the young Prince of Wales to his coronation (**ii**). Meanwhile, word comes to Queen Elizabeth that Richard and Buckingham have arrested her relatives— Rivers, Grey, and Vaughan. Frightened, she seeks sanctuary with the Archbishop of York (**iv**).

**ACT III.** When Buckingham and Richard accompany the young Prince to London, they meet Hastings and the young Duke of York. Richard, with Buckingham as accomplice, determines to play for the throne immediately, executing anyone who stands in the way (**i**). Lord Stanley, stepfather of Richmond, and Lord Hastings are called to a council in the Tower. Lord Stanley has been made fearful by foreboding dreams, but Hastings is happy that his enemies in the Queen's faction are to be executed. However, when Catesby, on orders from Richard, sounds Hastings out on the possibility of Richard's succeeding to the throne, Hastings recoils (**ii**). At the council in the Tower, Richard, because of this refusal, accuses Hastings of treason and orders his execution (**iv**). Richard then orders Buckingham to go with the Lord Mayor to the Guildhall and there to imply the bastardy of Edward and of Edward's children, to remind the people of Edward's unbridled lust, and to build up Richard as the true heir. Meanwhile, Richard intends to rid himself of Clarence's children (**v**). With hypocritical modesty and hesitancy, Richard allows Buckingham and the Lord Mayor to "draft" him to be King (**vii**).

**ACT IV.** Queen Elizabeth, the old Duchess, and Lady Anne hear that Richard is to be crowned king. Lady Anne must hurry to Westminster to be crowned Queen (**i**). After the coronation Richard suggests to Buckingham that they discuss the murders of the two sons of Edward, who have been placed in the Tower for their "protection." When Buckingham wavers at this point, Richard coldly snubs his request for advancement. Buckingham thereupon decides to fly from the court. Meanwhile, word arrives through Stanley that the Marquis of Dorset has fled to France to join Richmond. Richard, remembering Henry VI's prophecy that Richmond should be king, warns Stanley to have no dealings with his stepson (**ii**). Tyrrel, on Richard's orders, smothers the two Princes in the Tower. Richard, meanwhile, has forcibly detained the dim-witted son of Clarence and has forced a mean marriage on Clarence's daughter. Now Richard, having rid himself of Anne, intends to marry Elizabeth, daughter of King Edward. Word arrives that other English lords have fled to Richmond and that Buckingham and his Welsh are in the field (**iii**). Still exerting his fascination over women, Richard convinces Queen Elizabeth that she should allow him to marry her daughter. Plans for this marriage must be postponed, however, when news arrives that Richmond is on his way to England to claim the throne. As a precaution against the defection of Stanley, Richard holds his son, George Stanley, as hostage. News then arrives that Buckingham's army has been dispersed by floods and that the Duke has been taken prisoner (**iv**). Stanley sends word to Richmond, now landed in England, that George's being a hostage will prevent him from joining the enemies of Richard (**v**).

**ACT V.** After the execution of Buckingham (**i**) the two armies come together at Bosworth Field. The night before the battle, the ghosts of Richard's victims appear to him and to Richmond, cursing the former and encouraging the latter. After the leaders' orations to their armies, the battle is joined. Lord Stanley at the crucial moment refuses to bring up his forces to aid Richard, but Richard has not the time to execute George Stanley (**iii**). Although Richard fights valiantly (**iv**), he is defeated and killed by Richmond, who now intends to marry Princess Elizabeth and to unite the red and white roses into a consolidated kingdom (**v**).

# THE LIFE OF
# HENRY THE EIGHTH

## Cast of Characters

### Main Characters

KING HENRY VIII. Shakespeare handles Henry rather tenderly. Historically, of course, Henry, although a strong king, was a greedy lustful tryant. We see him here as leaning too strongly on Wolsey early in the play. Afterward, he deals fairly with everyone and sees to it that Archbishop Cranmer is not harmed by the jealousy of the council.

CARDINAL WOLSEY. Although Shakespeare gives Wolsey credit for being a scholar and for founding Oxford (IV, ii, 48-68), the Cardinal is the villain of the play. Greedy and ambitious, he allows nothing to stand in the way of his worldly hopes or of his desire to become Pope.

CRANMER, Archbishop of Canterbury. One of the first of the great Protestant bishops, Cranmer is accused by the council of being a schismatic; however, because he is honest, upright, and capable, he holds Henry's confidence.

QUEEN KATHARINE, wife to King Henry, afterwards divorced. Although Katharine is not a woman of action, hers is one of the few fully drawn portraits in the play. Obviously in love with Henry, she faces Wolsey defiantly in court; and when she falls from her high position, she remains sweet and forgiving.

ANNE BULLEN. Shakespeare depicts her as a beautiful maiden, whose face and bearing are queenly. To see her is to love her.

### Supporting Characters

CARDINAL CAMPEIUS, called in by Wolsey to assist in the divorce proceedings

CAPUCIUS, Ambassador from the Emperor Charles V

GARTER, King-at-Arms

The King's Council: LORD CHAMBERLAIN; LORD CHANCELLOR (Sir Thomas More); CROMWELL, earlier Wolsey's servant, afterwards Secretary of the Council; GARDINER, Bishop of Winchester, earlier Wolsey's choice as the King's Secretary; DUKE OF NORFOLK; DUKE OF SUFFOLK; EARL OF SURREY

LORD ABERGAVENNY and the DUKE OF BUCKINGHAM, arrested and executed for treason through Wolsey's malice

Courtiers: SIR ANTHONY DENNY; SIR HENRY GUILDFORD; BISHOP OF LINCOLN; SIR THOMAS LOVELL; LORD SANDYS (also called Sir William Sandys); SIR NICHOLAS VAUX

(Secretaries to Wolsey; GRIFFITH, gentleman-usher to Queen Katharine; Three Gentlemen, whose conversations fill in occurrences between scenes; DOCTOR BUTTS, physician to the King; Surveyor to the Duke of Buckingham, whose testimony convicts the Duke of treason; BRANDON, and a Sergeant-at-Arms; Doorkeeper of the Council Chamber; Porter and his man, comic relief; Page to Gardiner; a Crier; an old Lady, friend to Anne Bullen; PATIENCE, woman to Queen Katharine; Spirits; several Bishops; Lords and Ladies in the Dumb Shows; Women attending upon the Queen; Scribes; Officers; Guards; and other Attendants)

(Place: *London; Westminister; Kimbolton*)

BACKGROUND. Parts of this play may be the last published work from Shakespeare's hand. All dates of composition are highly conjectural, but some scholars prefer 1612. The only text is in the First Folio (1623). The sources are the *Chronicles* of Holinshed and Halle, and Foxe's *Actes and Monuments*.

## ACT BY ACT ANALYSIS

ACT I. Henry VIII and his Chancellor, Wolsey, have returned from a parley with the French King at the "Field of the Cloth of Gold." The Duke of Buckingham and the Lord Abergavenny, who have not been at the parley, discuss it with the Duke of Norfolk. Buckingham is indignant at the tremendous cost and seeming failure of the parley; for Wolsey, who arranged it, is particularly hated by the courtiers because of his greed, ambition, and lowly origin. Buckingham intends to denounce Wolsey to the King; but before he can reach Henry, Wolsey has him and Abergavenny arrested for treason on the testimony of Buckingham's surveyor (i). However, before the King can hear the surveyor's testimony, Queen Katharine enters and pleads the cause of the common people, from whom commissioners have been taking one-sixth of their substance. When the King becomes incensed at this state of affairs, Wolsey, who has been the one responsible for the tax, intends to remove it at the King's order but to take credit himself for its removal. From the testimony of the surveyor, Henry becomes convinced of Buckingham's guilt and orders him to trial (ii). Meanwhile Wolsey plans a supper, to which he has invited a large part of the Court (iii). When Henry, disguised, appears at the supper, he sees Anne Bullen and begins to fall in love with her (iv).

**ACT II.** After the trial of Buckingham, at which his servants have sworn against him, the great Duke is condemned and led away to be executed. Convinced that his downfall has come because he is next in line to the throne, Buckingham, before his death, forgives his enemies. Meanwhile, there are rumors that Wolsey is trying to separate Henry and Katharine, and that Cardinal Campeius has arrived to help him (i). Wolsey has worked on the King's conscience, pointing out that since Katharine has earlier been the wife of Henry's deceased brother Arthur, Henry's marriage to her is incestuous. The courtiers are certain that Wolsey is anxious to promote a marriage between Henry and the sister of the French King for reasons of policy. Wolsey and Campeius are appointed judges to decide the legality of Katharine's and Henry's marriage (ii). At the trial Katherine refuses to accept her old enemy Wolsey as a judge and stalks out of the hall. Stung by charges thrown at him by the Queen, Wolsey turns in feigned grief to Henry, who absolves him from ever having put the idea of divorce into his head. The Cardinals suggest that court be dissolved until such time as Katharine can be convinced not to carry out one of her threats: to appeal directly to the Pope. Henry is disturbed by the delay, but he breaks up the court for the time being (iv). Meanwhile, he has made Anne the Marchioness of Pembroke and settled a thousand pounds a year on her (iii).

**ACT III.** Wolsey, realizing for the first time that Anne is dangerous to his plans for the French marriage, makes a pact with Queen Katharine to help her regain her place (i). However, his plans came to naught when his letter intended for the Pope (asking the Holy Father to refuse to grant the divorce) and an inventory of his worldly goods fall by mistake into the King's hands. When, thereupon, Henry demands that he yield up the Great Seal, Wolsey realizes that his days at court are over, commends his servant Cromwell to the King, and prepares to leave his worldly honors. Meanwhile word has gotten around that Henry has secretly married Anne (ii).

**ACT IV.** After Cranmer and other judges have declared Henry's divorce from Katharine legal, Henry openly has Anne crowned Queen of England. However, rumors are thick that differences have arisen between Archbishop Cranmer and Cromwell on the one hand and Gardiner and some of the nobles on the other (i). Meanwhile, Katharine, who has been created Princess Dowager, sadly awaits death at Kimbolton. She hears that Wolsey has died of a broken heart at Leicester. (ii).

**ACT V.** Now the conspiracy against Cranmer crystallizes: in council Gardiner intends to accuse the Archbishop of heresy. However, Henry calls Cranmer to him, warns him of the plot, and gives him a ring which may be used to invoke the King directly when the council meets (i). Cranmer is left to cool his heels in the anteroom while the council is meeting, and Henry hides behind a curtain to observe the proceedings (ii). When the council unanimously votes to commit Cranmer to the Tower to await trial, the Archbishop produces the ring. The council realizes then that Henry is completely in sympathy with Cranmer. Soon afterwards Henry shows himself, demands that the council reverse itself, and names Cranmer as sponsor for the baptism of Princess Elizabeth, the infant daughter of Henry and Anne (iii). At the baptismal ceremony Cranmer predicts a great future for Queen Elizabeth and prophesies the accession of James I (v).

# TRAGEDIES

# OF

# WILLIAM SHAKESPEARE

# TITUS ANDRONICUS

## Cast of Characters

### Main Characters

AARON, an utterly villainous Moor, plays a double role as Tamora's public attendant and private lover.

BASSIANUS, a hot-headed young man, the new emperor's brother, refuses to give up his affianced bride.

CHIRON, Tamora's bestial son, proves himself as wicked as his mother.

DEMETRIUS, another son of Tamora, is like his brother, completely evil.

LAVINIA, the innocent bride of Bassianus and daughter of Titus, becomes the victim of a revolting plot.

LUCIUS, son of Titus Andronicus, proves himself a faithful son and able general.

MARCUS ANDRONICUS, brother of Titus, helps the old general in his plans for revenge.

SATURNINUS, the new emperor, a weak and revengeful man, turns against his benefactor, Titus Andronicus, and becomes the tool of Tamora and her consort.

TAMORA, Queen of the Goths, evil mother of an evil brood, seeks revenge but finds disaster.

TITUS ANDRONICUS, conquering Roman general, finds sorrow and despair instead of the "staff for his old age" for which he asked.

### Supporting Characters

AEMILIUS, a noble Roman
ALARBUS, son of Tamora
CAIUS, kinsman of Titus
MARTIUS, son of Titus

MUTIUS, son of Titus

NURSE, attendant on Tamora

PUBLIUS, son of Marcus

QUINTUS, son of Titus

SEMPRONIUS, kinsman of Titus

VALENTINE, kinsman of Titus

YOUNG LUCIUS, son of Lucius

(Captain, Messenger, Clown, Romans, Goths, Senators, Tribunes, Officer, Soldiers, Attendants)

(Place: *Rome, and the country near the city*)

BACKGROUND. A great deal of controversy has been raised among scholars about whether Shakespeare actually wrote this unpleasant play. Many scholars believe that Shakespeare merely made some slight revisions of an existing play. The title first appeared in the Stationers' Register in 1594. The probable source is a play, *Titus and Vespacia,* acted by Lord Strange's company of players in 1591.

## ACT BY ACT ANALYSIS

**ACT I.** Titus Andronicus returns to Rome after a lifetime of fighting against the enemies of his country. He finds Saturninus and Bassianus quarreling over their respective claims to the crown of Rome. Though Bassianus is engaged to Titus' daughter, Lavinia, the old soldier supports the claim of the elder brother, Saturninus, and rejects the offer made by his brother Marcus, speaking for the people of Rome, that he accept the crown himself. In order to bind the families more closely, he gives Lavinia in marriage to Saturninus. Titus has brought Tamora, Queen of the Goths, and her sons back to Rome as prisoners of war, together with the body of one of his own sons who has been killed in battle, the last of "five and twenty" of his children so to die. He gives Tamora's eldest son to be slain as a sacrifice at his dead son's tomb and turns the mother and her other sons over to the new emperor, Saturninus, who immediately falls in love with her. He begins to court her immediately.

Bassianus is enraged that his affianced bride has been taken from him, claims her at sword's point, and carries her away. His brothers side with him when Titus tries to prevent the flight.

Furious, the old man stabs his son, Mutius, who has been left to fight a rear guard action while the others escape. Lucius, another son, returns and defies his father when the old man demands that Lavinia be brought back to Saturninus. The new emperor, however, is arrogant. He resents having had to beg the throne from Andronicus and now he turns on the old man, scorns his daughter, and discredits his family. With her consent, he says, he will make Tamora his empress. The cunning Goth persuades Saturninus to pretend to forgive Titus and his family. He is too popular with the people, she says, for such a new emperor to quarrel with. She will find ways of taking revenge for the sacrifice of her son, but they must bide their time (i).

**ACT II.** Demetrius and Chiron, Tamora's bestial sons, both lust for Lavinia. While they are quarreling over her, they are interrupted by the Moor, Aaron, Tamora's black attendant and secret lover. He promises that he will aid them in their pursuit of Lavinia, if they will agree to share her charms and stop their quarrel. Otherwise, their mother will be disgraced and they themselves destroyed; for even the empress' sons cannot pursue a prince's wife with impunity. Their only chance, he tells them, is to seize the girl by force while the ladies of Rome are out in the forest with a hunting party. In such a plan he believes that Tamora, intent upon ultimate revenge, will not only give consent but lend actual assistance (i).

The hunting party, composed of the Roman court, meets in the forest (ii), while in a dark and lonely glade Aaron hides a bag of gold as part of his villainous scheme. When Tamora comes to meet her paramour, he puts off her attempts at love-making, and gives her a letter to deliver to Saturninus. He further instructs her to quarrel with Bassianus, who is approaching the glade, accompanied by his wife, Lavinia. While she is following out her instructions, the Moor runs to bring her sons. When Demetrius and Chiron appear, Tamora accuses Bassianus and Lavinia of attempting to kill her. The sons immediately murder Bassianus, and Tamora wishes to follow their action by stabbing Lavinia; but Demetrius and Chiron beg to be allowed to ravish her first, and leave, dragging their unfortunate victim with them. Aaron now arranges that two of Titus' sons discover the body of the murdered man, brings Saturninus to the scene, and "finds" the bag of gold. Saturninus has been given the letter which Aaron entrusted to Tamora. It tells of a plot to kill Bassianus and leave a bag of gold for the murderers. Saturninus immediately assumes that Titus' sons, discovered with the body, are guilty of the murder. He orders their torture and death (iii). Meanwhile, in another part of the forest, Tamora's foul sons have raped Lavinia, cut off her hands, and cut out her tongue, so that the mutilated girl cannot accuse them (iv).

**ACT III.** After Titus tries vainly to save his sons, Aaron comes to him with the message that if any of the Andronici will cut off a hand and send it to the emperor, the youths will be pardoned. Marcus, Titus, and Lucius (who has been banished for attempting to aid his brothers) all claim the honor; but when Marcus and Lucius go to find an axe, Titus cuts off one of his hands with a sword and gives it to the Moor. Aaron boasts to himself that the whole episode is a grotesque plot and that instead of receiving his sons, the father will receive their heads. When a messenger brings the heads and the dismembered hand, together with a contemptuous message from the emperor, Titus swears wildly that he will have revenge. He orders Lucius to go to the Goths and raise an army (i). Left alone with his brother and Lavinia, the old man broods and talks madly (ii).

**ACT IV.** Lavinia, by means of writing in the sand with her uncle's staff, is finally able to tell her family the names of her ravishers. Titus announces that he has a plan for securing revenge, and sends Young Lucius, his grandson, to deliver a message to Demetrius and Chiron (i). The message consists of the opening lines of a Horatian ode which translated means "He who is spotless in life and free from crime needs not Moorish bow and arrow." Aaron realizes that the father has discovered the perpetrators of the crime, but he keeps the information to himself. Now a frightened nurse appears before Aaron and the fiendish brothers, carrying a black-skinned baby. Tamora, she says, has just given birth to the child. Aaron saves the baby from the wrath of the brothers and kills the nurse to stop her mouth. He plans to substitute a fair-skinned child of a countryman for his black babe and to send his son to be reared by the Goths (ii). Titus, mad or pretending, searches throughout Rome to find Justice. He annoys the emperor by

shooting arrows into the air, bearing messages to the various
Roman gods begging for vengeance (**iii**). But when Saturninus
orders that Titus be dragged before him, Aemilius, a noble,
comes with the news that Lucius has gathered an overwhelming
force of Goths and plans to attack Rome. Saturninus is terrified,
but Tamora calms him. She will enchant the "old Andronicus"
so that he will call off his sons. She sends Aemilius to Lucius
asking for a parley to be held at Titus' house (**iv**).

**ACT V.** Lucius with his army of Goths captures Aaron and
his baby. Upon a promise that his son will be spared, Aaron
confesses all the horrible crimes of Tamora and her sons, and
boasts of his part in them. When Aemilius comes with Tamora's
request for a parley, Lucius agrees (**i**). Back in Rome, Tamora
and her sons come disguised to Titus' house. Though Titus
immediately recognizes her, the wily empress tries to convince
the old man that she is "Revenge," come with her ministers
to plot with Titus against his enemies. He pretends to believe
her, but when she leaves, he immediately has her sons bound
and gagged. The old father brings Lavinia to the scene; and,
after denouncing them for their evil deeds, he cuts their throats,
Lavinia holding a basin to catch their "guilty blood" (**ii**). Now
Lucius appears with Aaron, with whom he plans to confront
the empress. When the emperor and his court appear for the
parley, Titus, dressed as a cook, seats them at a banquet table.
Then the old man, justifying his act by the classical example of
Virginius, kills Lavinia before their eyes, that he may kill his
own grief. Next, Titus denounces Demetrius and Chiron as
the ravishers of his daughter. When Saturninus demands that
the guilty brothers be brought before him, Titus answers that
they are already there, baked in the pie upon which the empress
and the retinue have been feeding. Then Titus stabs Tamora,
and Saturninus, in turn, stabs Titus. Lucius kills Saturninus and
addresses the gathering throng of Romans. He shows the people
Aaron's body and tells them of the detestable acts of Tamora,
her sons, and her consort. After the people acclaim Lucius
as their emperor, the unrepentant Aaron is sentenced to torture
and death (**iii**).

# THE TRAGEDY OF ROMEO AND JULIET

## Cast of Characters

### *Main Characters*

ROMEO, member of the Montague family. Shakespeare characterizes him early in the play as a young man in love with the idea of love. As the action progresses, he becomes constantly more serious and more aware of his responsibility.

PARIS, related to Prince Escalus, and Capulet's choice for Juliet's hand. Paris' love for Juliet, next to the feud, is the chief obstacle in the way of the happy marriage of the lovers. Shakespeare portrays him as a perfectly normal, lusty young man, who shows great grief at the supposed death of his beloved.

MERCUTIO, a young, witty, carefree kinsman to Escalus. He is a triumph of characterization and one of the acting prizes of the play. His death forces Romeo to move against Tybalt.

TYBALT, fierce, almost feline, nephew to Lady Capulet. He seems to epitomize the baneful influence of the feud on the lovers. His death at the hands of Romeo furnishes an objectified obstacle to a fortunate outcome.

FRIAR LAURENCE, the Franciscan who is the confidant of the lovers and who marries them. His plan goes astray and leads directly to the lovers' deaths. At times he is resourceful, but his lethargy in getting to the tomb and his seeming cowardice after he gets there are partially responsible for the catastrophe.

JULIET, the other half of the "star-cross'd lovers." Only thirteen years old but sweet, loving, and faithful, she is one of the most admirable of Shakespearian heroines; yet she can be unbending when her emotions are involved.

## Supporting Characters

ESCALUS, Prince of Verona, arbiter of the feud

The Montagues: MONTAGUE, father of Romeo; BENVOLIO, nephew of Montague and close friend of Romeo; BALTHASAR, servant of Romeo; ABRAHAM, servant of Montague; LADY MONTAGUE, wife of Montague

The Capulets: CAPULET, father of Juliet; SAMPSON and GREGORY, servants of Capulet; an old man of the Capulet family; LADY CAPULET, wife of Capulet; the NURSE of Juliet, masterpiece of comic characterization; PETER, her servant

FRIAR JOHN, the ill-fated messenger from Friar Laurence to Romeo

(An Apothecary; three Musicians; Page to Paris; an Officer; Chorus; Citizens of Verona; Men and Women, kinsfolk to both houses; Maskers; Guards; Watchmen; and Attendants)

(Place: *Verona and Mantua*)

BACKGROUND. This tragedy was probably composed in 1594. There are five quartos: 1597, 1599, 1609, one undated, and 1637. The First Folio (1623) also contains a text taken from the third quarto. The text usually drawn upon is the one in the second quarto. The immediate sources for the play are to be found in Arthur Brooke's poem *The Tragicall Historye of Romeus and Juliet* (1562), and a tale in Painter's *Palace of Pleasure* (1567).

## ACT BY ACT ANALYSIS

**ACT I.** For the fourth time the streets of Verona are the scene of a brawl caused by the feud between the noble families of Capulet and Montague. This resumption of fighting has been caused by an altercation between servants of the feuding houses. When Benvolio, a Montague, attempts to stop the servants' brawling, he is attacked by Tybalt, a nephew of Capulet. Soon most of the members of both houses are involved. The Prince of Verona stops the mass fighting before anyone is hurt and warns the participants that on penalty of death there can be no repetition of the street brawls. When quiet again prevails, the Montagues realize that Romeo has not been present, but has been wandering by himself, wallowing in melancholy. When Romeo finally appears, he informs Benvolio that he is in love **(i)**. As Benvolio and Romeo stroll along the street, they meet a servant of Capulet's and discover that Capulet is having a supper and a ball; when they hear that Romeo's "fair Rosaline" will be present, they intend to mask and attend the function (ii). Meanwhile, Capulet has given Count Paris leave to sue for the hand of Juliet. Juliet tells her mother that she will be pleased to meet Paris and that she will obey her parents' wishes (iii). Romeo, Benvolio, and Mercutio set out for the entertainment, Mercutio keeping the others amused with his wonderful nonsense (iv). At the ball Romeo and Juliet meet, kiss, and fall in love, though Juliet is heartsick when her nurse tells her that her beloved is a Montague. When Tybalt recognizes Romeo and wishes to precipitate a fight, he is prevented by Capulet. Tybalt grudgingly defers to his uncle's wishes, but determines to avenge this insult to his family (v).

**ACT II.** Romeo gives his friends the slip, climbs the wall of Capulet's orchard (i), and waits for Juliet to appear at her window. When she does appear, the two confess their mutual love and determine to marry by stealth. Juliet is to send a message to Romeo by nine o'clock the next morning; meanwhile Romeo is to arrange for the wedding (ii). After being up all night, Romeo approaches Friar Laurence and asks him to perform the ceremony. The Friar, swept off his feet by Romeo's impetuosity, finally consents, hoping that through this marriage the feud may be ended (iii). The Nurse, acting as Juliet's messenger, arranges the details with Romeo. Juliet is to pretend to go to Friar Laurence's cell to be shriven (iv). Returning to the house the Nurse plagues Juliet for a while, then explains Romeo's plans (v). The lovers meet outside Friar Laurence's cell and enter to be married (vi).

**ACT III.** When Tybalt and Romeo meet on the street shortly after the marriage has been performed, the former challenges Romeo. Romeo, now that he is allied to the Capulets, attempts to placate him. However, Mercutio, not understanding Romeo's reluctance to fight, challenges Tybalt. Tybalt thereupon mortally wounds Mercutio under the arm of Romeo, who is attempting to stop the duel. Tybalt leaves; Mercutio dies; and, upon Tybalt's return to the scene, Romeo kills him. The Prince, angered by the death of Mercutio, his kinsman, and at the flouting of his orders, sentences Romeo to immediate exile (i).

Juliet, although saddened by the death of Tybalt and by the
banishment of Romeo, orders the Nurse to meet Romeo and to
ask him to come to her for the consummation of the marriage
(ii). In Friar Laurence's cell Romeo gives way to despair because of his banishment from Verona and Juliet. The Friar
cheers him and plans to send him to Mantua until such a time
as the marriage can be published and the Prince placated. When
the Nurse arrives with Juliet's message, Romeo determines to
see Juliet before he leaves for Mantua (iii). Meanwhile, Capulet
decides to marry Juliet to Paris within three days (iv). While
Capulet and Paris are discussing the plans, Romeo and Juliet
have consummated their marriage and have parted in the dawn.
Lady Capulet informs her daughter of the forthcoming alliance
with Paris, but Juliet spurns the proposal. Even when her
father threatens her, she remains adamant, and feels entirely
forsaken when the Nurse suggests that, since Romeo is gone,
she may as well commit bigamy and marry Paris (v).

**ACT IV.** Juliet, repairing to Friar Laurence for aid, meets
Paris in the Friar's cell. When the Count leaves, Juliet gives
way to despair. The Friar then proposes the following plan:
since the wedding is to take place on Thursday, on Wednesday
night Juliet shall swallow a potion which will make her appear
to be dead; meanwhile the Friar will send word to Romeo to
return from Mantua and to rescue his wife from the Capulet
tomb, where she undoubtedly will be buried (i). Capulet, goaded
by Juliet's opposition to his plans, now decides to move the
wedding up one day (ii), a plan which necessitates Juliet's
drinking the potion instantly. She sends the Nurse out of the
room and drinks the potion, not without misgivings (iii). In
the morning when the Nurse goes to awaken Juliet (iv), she finds
her mistress lifeless. Friar Laurence and Paris arrive, but the
wedding plans must be changed to funeral plans (v).

**ACT V.** Unfortunately, Friar Laurence's messenger to Romeo,
Friar John, has been detained by quarantine (ii). In consequence
Balthasar arrives in Mantua ahead of the Friar and tells Romeo
of Juliet's supposed death. Thereupon, Romeo purchases poison
and determines to slay himself in Juliet's tomb (i). Friar
Laurence must now also hasten to the tomb to prevent disaster
(ii). When Romeo and Balthasar arrive at the tomb, they find

Paris already there mourning for Juliet. Reluctantly, Romeo is forced to meet a challenge from Paris and to kill his rival. Lying beside Juliet, Romeo swallows the poison and dies. Friar Laurence arrives in the tomb too late to prevent the tragedy running its full course: when Juliet awakens, the Friar hears someone approaching and retires. Juliet, left alone, discovers the dead Romeo and kills herself with her husband's dagger. The Prince and the members of the feuding families arrive. Over the bodies of the dead lovers, the feud is ended. The Prince promises impartial but strict justice to all concerned (iii).

# JULIUS CAESAR

## Cast of Characters

### *Main Characters*

JULIUS CAESAR, conquering Roman general, though a mighty soldier, is swayed by superstition and allows flattery to carry him to his death.

MARCUS BRUTUS is the only one of the conspiring nobles whose motives are essentially pure. His high idealism is used by Caesar's envious enemies to further their own selfish purposes. Even his enemy, Antony, calls him "the noblest Roman of them all."

MARCUS ANTONIUS (usually called Mark Antony in the play) sets himself to avenge Caesar's death. His shrewd and wily manipulations are paralleled by Brutus' lofty but shortsighted idealism.

M. AEMILIUS LEPIDUS, though he becomes one of the ruling triumvirs, together with Octavius Caesar and Antony, is "a slight man" who is exploited by his stronger partners.

CAIUS CASSIUS represents the greed and envy motivating most of the conspirators. His "itching palm" presents a striking contrast when paralleled with Brutus' basic nobility.

CASCA, another conspirator against Caesar, hates the ordinary citizenry, yet is jealous when the people acclaim Caesar.

OCTAVIUS CAESAR, Julius Caesar's heir, joins with Antony and Lepidus to lead forces against Brutus and to share with them the title of triumvir.

### *Supporting Characters*

ARTEMIDORUS, a rhetorician

DECIUS BRUTUS, a conspirator against Julius Caesar

CALPURNIA, wife of Julius Caesar

YOUNG CATO, friend of Brutus and Cassius

CICERO, a senator

METELLUS CIMBER, a conspirator against Julius Caesar

CINNA, a conspirator against Julius Caesar

CINNA, a poet

CLAUDIUS, a servant of Brutus

CLITUS, a servant of Brutus

DARDANIUS, a servant of Brutus

FLAVIUS, a tribune

CAIUS LIGARIUS, a conspirator against Julius Caesar

LUCILIUS, friend of Brutus and Cassius

LUCIUS, servant of Brutus

MARULLUS, a tribune

MESSALA, a friend of Brutus and Cassius

PINDARUS, a servant of Cassius

POPILIUS LENA, a senator

PORTIA, wife of Brutus

PUBLIUS, a senator

STRATO, a servant of Brutus

TITINIUS, a friend of Brutus and Cassius

TREBONIUS, a conspirator against Julius Caesar

VARRO, a servant of Brutus

VOLUMNIUS, a friend of Brutus and Cassius

(A Soothsayer, Another Poet, Senators, Citizens, Guards, Attendants, Messengers)

(Place: *Rome; the vicinity of Sardis; the vicinity of Philippi*)

BACKGROUND: This play was probably composed about 1599, though the First Folio (1623) is the earliest printed edition. In so far as the play is historical, it is drawn from Thomas North's translation of Plutarch's *Lives*. In fact, in many passages Shakespeare merely rendered North's prose into blank verse. Simple in its dramatic structure, it is one of the relatively few Shakesperean plays that are not encumbered with secondary elements and subplots.

## ACT BY ACT ANALYSIS

**ACT I.** Julius Caesar is returning victorious to Rome. His extreme popularity with the ordinary citizenry displeases a faction of Roman nobles, who both fear Caesar's ambition and envy his growing power (i). These nobles, led by Cassius, agree to plot against Caesar. When the great general enters Rome, he is warned by a soothsayer to "beware the ides of March," and his superstitious nature is troubled, though the populace loudly applauds him and three times offers him an emperor's crown (ii). The plotting nobles, too, see supernatural omens, but Cassius interprets them as warnings of Caesar's ambitions. In order to perfect their plot, the nobles need support from the idealistic Brutus, Cassius' brother-in-law. This support they plan to gain by trickery (iii).

**ACT II.** The plotters, led by Cassius and Casca, visit Brutus in his orchard by night. He has been brooding there alone, aroused by false letters denouncing Caesar—letters really sent by the plotters. Though Brutus finally agrees that Caesar must die, he refuses to sanction the death of Caesar's strongest supporters, Marcus Antonius (or Mark Antony as he is usually called). "We should be called purgers," he says, "not murderers." When the other plotters leave, Brutus is troubled, but refuses to tell even his wife, Portia, what is troubling him (i). Early the next morning, Caesar is greatly worried by the supernatural happenings throughout the city. His wife, Calpurnia, who has muttered of evil during her troubled sleep, begs her husband to stay away from the Capitol. Her argument is reinforced by the priests and "augerers." But Decius Brutus, one of the plotters, by playing upon the great man's vanity, finally persuades him to go (ii). Outside, a rhetorician, Artemadorus, waits with a letter again warning Caesar (iii), while Portia, nearly frantic with worry, sends a messenger to find out what is happening at the Capitol (iv).

**ACT III.** Both the soothsayer and Artemadorous deliver their warnings, but Caesar will not listen to the soothsayer and does not read the letter Artemadorus thrusts into his hand. At the Capitol, Trebonius draws Antony away while the plotters crowd around Caesar under pretext of presenting a petition. When Caesar refuses to grant the request, the plotters stab him, Casca striking first. Now Brutus makes his great mistake. He allows Antony to speak Caesar's funeral oration, pledging him only to refrain from speaking ill of the conspirators. Brutus intends to speak first to the people, explaining the reasons why

Caesar's death was necessary (**i**). The people at first accept Brutus' explanation, but when the wily Antony speaks (though he holds to his promise), his cunningly contrived oratory arouses the mob's fury against the plotters. The seeds of revolt planted, Antony goes to meet with Octavius Caesar and Lepidus, to raise forces against the plotters (**ii**), while the mob disperses to attack the houses of the conspirators (**iii**).

**ACT IV.** Antony meets with Octavius and Lepidus. They plan to kill those of the plotters still in Rome and to raise troops against Brutus and his followers, who are camped with their army at Sardi (**i**). In this camp, Brutus quarrels with Cassius (**ii**), who has shown his true character by accepting bribes, by oppressing the peasants, and by other acts of downright dishonesty. Cassius, however, wins Brutus over to the extent that Brutus admits that he was "ill-tempered too." Finally Brutus tells Cassius the real cause for his bad humor—he has learned that his wife, Portia, has committed suicide. Cassius is deeply moved. Perhaps for this reason, he finally agrees when Brutus proposes to attack the enemy at Philippi, instead of following Cassius' battle plan, which calls for a purely defensive strategy. Left alone in his tent, Brutus is visited by his "evil spirit," the ghost of Caesar. They shall, the ghost tells Brutus, meet again at Philippi (**iii**).

**ACT V.** On the plains of Philippi, Antony and the conspirators, led by Brutus, meet. A parley is arranged, but results in nothing but mutual recriminations. Though ready for battle, Cassius is much troubled by evil omens. Brutus, too, has misgivings, but prepares to fight (**i**), and sends Messala with a message to his legions, ordering them to attack (**ii**). For Cassius the battle goes badly, and he believes himself surrounded. Despairing, he sends Titinius to find if troops on a hill above them are Antony's, then takes the word of his bondsman, Pindarus, that his scout has been captured. Believing all is lost, he commands Pindarus to stab him and dies upon the same sword he used against Caesar. Actually, Titinius has met Messala, sent by Brutus with word that the legions of both Antony and Octavius have been overthrown (**iii**). But now the tide of battle turns against Brutus. Young Cato is killed and Lucilius is captured (**iv**). Brutus, who has twice more seen the ghost of Caesar, believes his time has come. Rather than risk capture, he runs against a sword held by one of his followers. The now victorious Antony eulogizes his fallen enemy as the only one of the conspirators not motivated by envy. He plans to bury Brutus with full honors (v).

# THE TRAGEDY OF HAMLET, PRINCE OF DENMARK

## Cast of Characters

### *Main Characters*

CLAUDIUS, King of Denmark, and Hamlet's uncle. The villain of the tragedy, Claudius is not entirely a heartless monster. Constantly stung by his conscience, Claudius finds himself enmeshed further and further in the web that he has spun when he murdered his brother and married his brother's widow.

HAMLET, the protagonist of the tragedy. More nonsense has been written about Hamlet than about any other of Shakespeare's characters. His character has been variously interpreted both in books and on the stage. He most certainly is not mad; he specifically mentions (I, v) that he intends to put on "an antic disposition." Also the notion that Hamlet's is the tragedy of the man who cannot make up his mind has been exploded by enlightened critical opinion. Probably the exigencies of the five-act structure and the necessity of creating a full-length play are responsible for Hamlet's vacillations. Shakespeare, in order to string out the action, must motivate each failure of Hamlet to avenge his father. He has motivated these failures carefully, if not always credibly. One must remember, further, that much of the material for the play was filtered from Saxo Grammaticus' *Historica Danica* through a lost revenge play on the subject (probably by Kyd); that the pseudo-madness in Saxo is motivated; and that the Ghost, the play within a play, and the fencing scene in all probability come from the lost play, which Shakespeare undoubtedly reworked. From internal evidence we can see Hamlet as a sensitive, yet active, young man. Cf. Ophelia's characterization of him (III, i).

POLONIUS, a fussy old courtier, father of Ophelia and Laertes. He functions in the tragedy as the butt of Hamlet's jokes, and, through his death, as the final motivation for the exile of Hamlet to England.

HORATIO, close friend of and obviously a foil for Hamlet. Hamlet characterizes him as a stoic, a man whose imagination is not his master. His stoicism complements and sets off Hamlet's imaginativeness.

LAERTES, son of Polonius and brother of Ophelia. Also a foil for Hamlet, Laertes is quick to demand revenge for his father's murder and is immediately ready to carry it out.

GERTRUDE, Hamlet's mother and wife of Claudius. Gertrude's participation in Claudius' murder of the elder Hamlet is never quite clear. The Ghost advises Hamlet not to harm his mother; yet, at various places in the play she seems cognizant of, if not an accessory to, the murder.

OPHELIA, daughter of Polonius and sister of Laertes. One of the sweetest and most helpless of Shakespeare's tragic women, Ophelia also has a function as a foil to Hamlet: her real madness quite obviously sets off Hamlet's feigned madness.

## *Supporting Characters*

BERNARDO and MARCELLUS, officers; FRANCISCO, a soldier.

CORNELIUS and VOLTIMAND, ambassadors from Claudius to Fortinbras

FORTINBRAS, Prince of Norway, who inherits the Danish Kingdom

GHOST of Hamlet's father

GUILDENSTERN and ROSENCRANZ, school friends of Hamlet, used by Claudius to spy on his nephew

OSRIC, epitome of the fawning flatterer

(A gentleman; REYNALDO, servant to Polonius; a Priest; Players; Two Clowns, grave-diggers, famous comic figures; a Norwegian Captain; English Ambassadors; Lords; Ladies; Officers; Soldiers; Sailors; Messengers; Attendants)

(Place: *Elsinore, Denmark*)

BACKGROUND. The date of the composition of *Hamlet* is highly conjectural. Most opinion leans toward 1600 or 1601. There are three distinct texts: the mangled first quarto of 1603, the better second quarto of 1604, and the First Folio version (1623). All three are ordinarily used, with the greatest reliance being placed on the First Folio text. The ultimate source of *Hamlet* is to be found in the *Historica Danica* by Saxo Grammaticus (c. 1200); the tale was adapted by Belleforest in his *Histories Tragiques* (1576). The real difficulty in ascertaining the direct source of the tragedy lies in the fact that there is a lost play on the subject between Belleforest's tale and Shakespeare's play.

## ACT BY ACT ANALYSIS

**ACT I.** Denmark is in a turmoil. The elder Hamlet, King of Denmark, has died suddenly and mysteriously. When Prince Hamlet is summoned from school at Wittenberg for his father's funeral, he discovers that his uncle Claudius has succeeded to the throne and has, with unseemly haste, married Gertrude, Hamlet's mother and widow of the late King. Hamlet wishes to return to the University, but Claudius refuses permission; however, when Laertes asks the King's consent to go to Paris, it is immediately given (**ii**). In addition, there are rumors of an invasion of Denmark by young Fortinbras of Norway, whose father the elder Hamlet has slain in battle. Furthermore, the guards of a section of the battlements at Elsinore have been nightly disturbed by a ghost which strangely resembles the late King. They have informed Horatio, who watches with them and sees the ghost, which, however, refuses to speak to him. Horatio, in turn, determines to bring Hamlet to the battlements; for he feels that the apparition may speak to the Prince (**i**). In the meantime, Hamlet is revolted by his mother's incestuous marriage and is nearly ready to renounce life. When Horatio tells him of the apparition, he excitedly consents to share the watch this night (**ii**). On the battlements the Ghost appears to Hamlet, and, drawing him away from the others (**iv**), speaks to him. It tells him that it is his father's spirit and informs him that his father has been treacherously slain by Claudius, who has poured poison in the father's ears. Hamlet swears revenge on Claudius, and, without sharing his information with his companions, tells them that he intends to play mad; he then enjoins them to strict secrecy (**v**). Meanwhile, Laertes and Polonius forbid Hamlet's beloved Ophelia to trust the Prince or even to see him again in private. Laertes leaves for France after receiving some commonplace advice from his father (**iii**).

**ACT II.** Hamlet's apparent madness has upset the court. When Polonius discovers that Hamlet has acted in a peculiar manner while with Ophelia, he is sure that the Prince has gone mad from love (**i**). Polonius springs his discovery on Claudius; and the two plan to bring Hamlet and Ophelia together, to hide, and to watch the reaction of the Prince. Meanwhile, a number of people arrive at court: the Ambassadors to Norway, who bring word that Fortinbras has no hostile designs on Denmark, but merely intends to pass through Denmark to attack Poland; and Rosencrantz and Guildenstern, two school friends of Hamlet, who have been sent for by Claudius to act as spies on his nephew. With these friends a band of players has also arrived. Hamlet determines to use the players to make certain that the Ghost has not been a devil in disguise, and that his uncle is really the murderer (**ii**).

**ACT III.** The King and Polonius spring their trap on Hamlet, but he spurns Ophelia. Claudius, convinced that love is not the cause of Hamlet's madness, decides to send him to England under the supervision of Guildenstern and Rosencrantz (**i**). Before this plan can be effected, Hamlet, who has revised the players' tragedy to include a sequence directly drawn from the crimes of Claudius and Gertrude, is convinced of Claudius' guilt by watching his uncle's actions during the performance; he now intends to consummate his revenge (**ii**). Meanwhile, when Hamlet is summoned to his mother's chamber, Polonius offers to hide himself in the room to listen to Hamlet's conversation with Gertrude. On his way to see his mother, Hamlet discovers Claudius unprotected while at his prayers; but he refuses to murder his uncle now because he feels that, being at prayer, Claudius' soul will go directly to Heaven. (Claudius had killed the elder Hamlet without giving him a chance to make his confession or to receive unction) (**iii**). Hamlet's threatening actions frighten the Queen so that she calls out for help. When there is an answering cry behind the arras, Hamlet, thinking the cry comes from his uncle, stabs Polonius, who is hiding there. Hamlet's words and gestures confirm his mother's opinion that he is mad; for when he sees the Ghost stride into the chamber, she is unable to perceive it. However, he receives her promise to be neutral toward him (**iv**).

**ACT IV.** Hamlet's murder of Polonius makes his departure for England imperative (**i**). Rosencrantz and Guildenstern accompany him, with a sealed request that the King of England execute the Prince upon his arrival (**iii**). Meanwhile, Ophelia is driven mad by the knowledge that her beloved has killed her father (**v**), and dies—probably a suicide (**vii**). Laertes returns from Paris and demands revenge for his father's murder (**vi**). Claudius suggests a fencing match between Laertes and Hamlet, who has escaped from his ship and is returning to Denmark. Laertes suggests that he anoint his own sword with a deadly poison, and Claudius offers to furnish a poisoned chalice, should the sword fail (**vii**).

**ACT V.** At Ophelia's burial Laertes, with a great show of grief, throws himself into her grave. Hamlet, who has just arrived in Denmark and who is secretly watching the funeral, rushes out and grapples with him. However, Claudius separates them; and, together with Laertes, he perfects the plan for the death of Hamlet (**i**). Hamlet has just finished telling Horatio that he has exchanged the letter in the hands of Rosencrantz and Guildenstern for one that calls for their own deaths, when he receives the supposedly friendly challenge from Laertes. He accepts the challenge in spite of the misgivings of Horatio. Hamlet touches Laertes twice before the latter finally wounds him. In the scuffle the swords are exchanged, and Hamlet wounds Laertes with the poisoned sword. Unknowingly, Gertrude drinks from the poisoned cup; but before she and Laertes die, they inform Hamlet of the complete perfidy of the King. Hamlet, thereupon, kills Claudius with the poisoned sword. Hamlet then dies in the arms of Horatio, swearing his friend to remain alive and to tell the truth of the story. The English Ambassadors enter with news of the execution of Rosencrantz and Guildenstern. Then when Fortinbras arrives from the war with Poland, he, by default, inherits the throne of Denmark and intends to restore order in the state (**ii**).

# TROILUS AND CRESSIDA

## Cast of Characters

### Main Characters

TROILUS, a son of Priam, finds that pledges of undying love cannot always be believed.

CRESSIDA, Calchas' daughter, proves that she is wanton in love.

PANDARUS, a leering go-between for his niece, Cressida.

HECTOR, Troilus' elder brother, the champion of the Trojans, is treacherously slain by Achilles.

ACHILLES, the Greek warrior, sulks in his tent from vanity, then murders unarmed Hector.

ULYSSES, another mighty Greek, is not fooled by Cressida's smiles and gay games.

AJAX, a brutish Greek, is used as an instrument to prick Achilles' vanity.

DIOMEDES, a sly fellow, loses no time in wooing Cressida.

PATROCLUS, a foul-talking, scurrilous companion to Achilles.

THERSITES, an even worse rogue than Patroclus, and the companion of Ajax.

AGAMEMNON, the leader of the Greek army.

NESTOR, a wise old Greek commander.

AENEAS, a Trojan commander who is kept busy as a messenger.

CALCHAS, a traitorous Trojan priest, gets his daughter delivered to him in an exchange of prisoners.

### Supporting Characters

ALEXANDER, Cressida's servant

ANDROMACHE, Hector's wife

ANTENOR, a Trojan warrior

CASSANDRA, the mad prophetess, daughter of Priam

DEIPHOBUS, Priam's son

HELEN, Menelaus' wife

HELENUS, Priam's son

MARGARELON, Priam's son

MENELAUS, Agamemnon's brother

PARIS, Priam's son

PRIAM, King of Troy

SERVANTS, to Troilus, Paris, and Diomedes

(Greek and Trojan Soldiers, Attendants)

(Place: *The city of Troy and the Greek camp before it*)

BACKGROUND. This play was composed in 1601 and was first printed in 1609. Since the story of Troy is so widely treated in literature, Shakespeare had innumerable sources at his command. The main sources, though, have been well established; the love story is drawn from Chaucer's *Troilus and Criseyde,* and the scenes of fighting and the camps are from Caxton's *Recuyell of the Historyes of Troye* and from Homer.

## ACT BY ACT ANALYSIS

**ACT I.** During a stalemate in the Trojan war, Troilus, a noble Trojan youth, has fallen in love with Cressida. Pandarus, her kinsman, has been acting as a go-between for the young couple (**i**). At every opportunity Pandarus praises the virtues of Troilus, and Cressida admits that she thinks much more highly of him than she has previously admitted (**ii**). Meanwhile, in the Greek camp Agamemnon, the Greek leader, and his followers are discussing the unsatisfactory state of war after seven long years of siege. The chief difficulty seems to lie in the lack of discipline among the warriors; and Agamemnon cites the examples of Achilles and Patroclus, who are lolling in their tents, refusing, from vanity, to fight the Trojans. This insubordination has infected the rest of the army, including Ajax and his follower, Thersites. Now Aeneas comes from Troy, bearing a challenge from Hector, the Trojan champion, to meet any Greek in single combat. Nestor and Ulysses decide that Achilles, the natural one to accept the challenge, shall not do so, since it will make him even more vain. They plan, therefore, to choose the champion by lottery, and to arrange it so that the "blockish" Ajax will be selected (**iii**).

**ACT II.** A proclamation concerning the challenge is circulated throughout the Greek camp (**i**). Achilles continues to sulk in his tent, and the other Greeks build up the ego of Ajax by telling him that he is a better man than Achilles (**iii**). Back in Troy, Hector thinks longingly of peace and suggests that the Trojans take advantage of a Greek peace offer and return the captive Helen to her people. Only his sister, mad Cassandra the prophetess, agrees with him (**ii**).

**ACT III.** Pandarus finally arranges a meeting between Troilus and Cressida (**i**), and the young lovers pledge undying love (**ii**). But in the Greek camp, Calchas (Cressida's father, a Trojan priest who has deserted to the Greeks) asks that a newly captured Trojan, Antenor, be given in an exchange of prisoners for Cressida. This request is agreed to. Meanwhile, Achilles is being roundly snubbed by his companions; and, in a deeply pensive mood, he asks that Hector be invited to meet him in a truce after the combat between Hector and Ajax (**iii**).

**ACT IV.** The terms of the exchange of prisoners are carried out and Diomedes brings Antenor to Troy (**i**). Troilus, who is with Cressida at Pandarus' house, learns of the approach of the exchange party, and though she is crushed, she goes meekly enough with Aeneas, who has brought him the news (**ii**); and the young lover is chosen as the one to tell Cressida that she must submit to the exchange terms (**iii**). Touchingly, the lovers again swear to be true forever and exchange love tokens—Troilus gives Cressida a sleeve—as pledge of their undying love (**iv**). But no sooner has Cressida arrived in the Greek camp than she is playing kissing games of welcome with the Greeks, much to the disgust of Ulysses. Now Ajax and Hector meet in combat, but after one indecisive clash, Hector asks to stop. He cannot, he says, stomach fighting against his own nephew. As the others prepare for a feast to celebrate the truce, Troilus, who has accompanied the Trojans to the Greek camp, finds that Diomedes has been busily wooing Cressida in Menelaus' tent (**v**).

**ACT V.** As the Greeks and Trojans march to the banquet of the truce, Diomedes suddenly tells the others that he has important business and cannot accompany them (**i**). Troilus—accompanied by Ulysses, who is convinced of Cressida's unworthiness—follows Diomedes and watches Cressida coquet with him before Calchas' tent. She finally gives him Troilus' love token and agrees to submit to him later. Troilus is shattered by what he has seen, and vows to avenge himself on Diomedes in battle. He hurries home to Troy, where Hector is already again preparing for war (**ii**), despite the warnings of mad Cassandra and Andromache, his wife (**iii**). The war begins, and Troilus meets Diomedes (**iv**), who is victorious in the encounter and brings Troilus' horse to a servant to send as a present to the false Cressida (**v**). Ajax, whose friend Troilus has killed, roars about looking for the youth; and when he appears with Diomedes, Troilus engages them both at once (**vi**). In another part of the plain Achilles after a long search (**vii**), finds Hector, after the Trojan hero has disarmed, and treacherously kills him. Agamemnon, hearing the news, sends for Achilles, and the battle ends (**ix**). Troilus, bringing the news of Hector's death to the Trojans, swears undying revenge and curses Pandarus for his part in his misfortune (**x**).

# OTHELLO,
# THE MOOR OF VENICE

## Cast of Characters

### Main Characters

OTHELLO, a Moor in the military service of Venice. Othello is one of Shakespeare's great tragic protagonists. Originally a straight-forward, direct, not-too-subtle character, he becomes a monster of jealousy through the machinations of Iago. Because of his very nobleness, he is easily gulled by Iago; but at the end of the play he is all that he was before the catastrophe and more, having been chastened by suffering and purified by tragedy. Shakespeare undoubtedly had his own conception of Moors, strengthened by his source material; but he has remarkably transcended the source. Othello has some of the almost animal savagery of the pagan: he leaps quickly from thought to deed; but he is never merely a type.

IAGO, an ensign, a villain. Iago is one of the great problem characters in Shakespeare. Because he seems to lack adequate motivation to carry him to the lengths he reaches, he has been often interpreted, and even more often played, as the devil's representative, a satanic figure without conscience or remorse. However, if one follows his speeches closely, he recognizes that Iago has no notion in the beginning how far his villainy will go. Despising Othello as stupidly good and hating Cassio for superseding him as lieutenant, Iago seems to be merely an opportunist. Having once begun his mischief, he cannot extricate himself from the web he has spun. As he finds that one step in villainy inevitably leads to the next, he begins to enjoy his machinations and the feeling of power they afford him. The other motivations that he mentions—jealousy of Othello and Emilia and of Cassio and Emilia, and his own lust for Desdemona—are perhaps merely rationalizations.

CASSIO, an honorable lieutenant. Obviously a foil for Iago, Cassio is all that men believe Iago to be: honest and trustworthy. Although he is not a paragon of virtue, he is an admirable man.

DESDEMONA, daughter of Brabantio and wife of Othello. Desdemona is one of Shakespeare's memorable women. Less shadowy than Ophelia, less strongwilled than Lady Macbeth, she is primarily a sweet-tempered woman deeply in love with her husband. Like Othello she is no match for the devious Iago: every move that she makes from noble motives plays directly into his hands. Her pity for Cassio leads to her death.

EMILIA, wife of Iago. Sharp-tongued, wise in the ways of the world, Emilia is a foil to Desdemona. She is evidently in love with her husband; and this love, in spite of her experience, blinds her to Iago's real character and purposes. She, like Othello, nobly redeems herself at the end; by repudiating her husband, she suffers death at his hands.

### Supporting Characters

BIANCA, a courtesan, in love with Cassio

BRABANTIO, a senator, father to Desdemona. Probably reasonably enough, Brabantio welcomes Othello to his home as an honored guest, but objects to him as a son-in-law because he is a Moor.

DUKE OF VENICE, who orders Othello to Cyprus

GRATIANO, brother to Brabantio, a noble Venetian

LODOVICO, kinsman to Brabantio, a noble Venetian

MONTANO, a governor of Cyprus before Othello

RODERIGO, a gulled gentleman. Completely stupid, Roderigo does Iago's dirty work for him, while Iago keeps his hand in Roderigo's pocket by promising him that he will eventually possess Desdemona.

(Senators; Clown, servant to Othello; Gentlemen of Cyprus; Sailors; Officers; Messenger; Herald, Musicians, and Attendants)

(Place: *Venice; a seaport in Cyprus*)

BACKGROUND. The probable date is 1604. The two texts are the first quarto (1622) and the First Folio (1623); both are used in modern versions. The source is a tale in the *Hecatommithi* (1565) by Giraldi Cinthio.

## ACT BY ACT ANALYSIS

**ACT I.** Othello has secretly married Desdemona, daughter of Senator Brabantio. Meanwhile, Iago is incensed at Othello for appointing Michael Cassio instead of Iago as his lieutenant.

To have some revenge on Othello, Iago stirs up Roderigo, who has been rejected by Desdemona, to go to Brabantio at night and report the marriage. Brabantio immediately dresses and goes to seek Othello and Desdemona (i). Meanwhile, Iago, who has sneaked away to join Othello, warns his chief that Brabantio is searching for him. Cassio arrives with the news that the Duke wishes to see Othello immediately; but while the Moor is on his way to the council chamber, he meets Brabantio, who accuses him of drugging his daughter and orders him seized. When Othello informs Brabantio that he has been sent for by the Duke, Brabantio proposes that the Duke be made the judge of the case (ii). At the council chamber the Duke hears that the Turks are threatening Cyprus; and as soon as Brabantio and Othello arrive, he orders Othello to lead the Venetian forces against the Turks. Before Othello can answer, Brabantio breaks in with his grief for his daughter's marriage. After Othello nobly and simply defends himself from the charge of sorcery, Desdemona enters and confirms her husband's story. Brabantio has no more to say, and Othello prepares to leave for Cyprus. He receives permission for Desdemona to follow him there and leaves her with "honest" Iago. Iago then speaks privately with Roderigo, tells him to raise more money, and promises him that he shall still enjoy Desdemona. Iago, now that the wheels are in motion, remembers that there has been some talk about illicit relations between Othello and Emilia, Iago's wife. Iago decides that he will make the Moor suspect that Desdemona is having an affair with Cassio (iii).

**ACT II.** Near Cyprus the Turkish fleet has been destroyed by a storm. First Cassio, then Iago and Desdemona, and finally Othello arrive on the island. Iago calls Roderigo's attention to a private conversation between Cassio and Desdemona; then he suggests that Roderigo provoke a quarrel with Cassio, who has been made Captain of the Guard. The resulting brawl, Iago feels, will bring Cassio into disgrace. Iago, who now suspects an affair between Cassio and Emilia and who feels a lust for Desdemona, intends to disgrace both Cassio and Othello (i). His first step is to get Cassio drunk; when Roderigo insults Cassio, Cassio strikes Roderigo and then wounds Montano, who tries to stop the brawl. Othello, highly incensed at

Cassio, deprives him of his offices. When Iago suggests to
Cassio that he apply to Desdemona to intercede with Othello,
Cassio falls into the trap. Iago now intends to convince Othello
that Desdemona's intercession for Cassio arises out of her love
for the young man (**iii**).

**ACT III.** Cassio first asks Emilia to go to Desdemona for
him; Desdemona, in turn, immediately pleads with Othello to
restore Cassio's honors and good name (**i**). While Cassio talks
to Desdemona about his problems, Iago and Othello come
surreptitiously on the pair; Iago uses this occasion to pour
the first drops of the poison of jealousy into the Moor's ears.
Unwilling to believe Desdemona unfaithful, Othello is troubled
by Iago's innuendoes. He insists that he will not believe without
visual proof. Iago's opportunity to furnish this proof comes
when Othello unwittingly drops a handkerchief handed him by
Desdemona. Emilia picks it up and gives it to her husband;
Iago intends to hide it in Cassio's lodgings. He then returns
to Othello, who demands ocular proof of Desdemona's unfaithfulness. Iago first tells the Moor that he has heard Cassio
speak of Desdemona in his sleep. He then insists that he has
seen Cassio with Desdemona's handkerchief, and whips Othello's
jealousy to such a pitch that the Moor swears to avenge himself
on his wife (**iii**). When Othello asks Desdemona for the handkerchief, she hesitates, then says that she has lost it. The Moor
stalks out angrily. Cassio, who has found the handkerchief in
his chamber and likes it, gives it to Bianca and asks her to have
it copied for him (**iv**).

**ACT IV.** Iago's next move is to talk with Cassio about Bianca,
having first placed Othello nearly out of earshot. The Moor
hears just enough to be convinced that the two are talking about
Desdemona. When Bianca enters with Desdemona's handkerchief, Othello is fully convinced of his wife's guilt and
intends to murder her this night; he then orders Iago to kill
Cassio. Lodovico, who now appears with letters recalling
Othello to Venice and making Cassio governor in his place, is
startled at the queerness of the Moor's behavior (**i**). Desdemona
is also tremendously upset when Othello accuses her of being a
whore; she has no notion, of course, what he is talking about.

Iago then suggests to Roderigo that he kill Cassio before Cassio has the opportunity to assume the governorship (**ii**).

**ACT V.** When Roderigo attacks Cassio, the latter wounds him; but Iago comes up from behind and wounds Cassio in the leg. When others arrive on the scene, Iago, who has hidden, re-enters, and, pretending to be indignant, kills the wounded Roderigo before he has a chance to talk (**i**). Meanwhile, in the bedchamber Othello smothers Desdemona. When Emilia enters, and, thunderstruck, asks the reason for the slaying, Othello declares that his wife has been a whore and that Iago has known it. Emilia's screams call Iago, Montano, and Gratiano to the scene. Emilia, beginning to realize that her husband is implicated in the murder, tells the truth about the handkerchief. Othello rushes at Iago but before he can reach him, Iago stabs Emilia. When the representatives of the Senate enter with more proof of Iago's villainy, Othello wounds Iago and stabs himself. As the Moor dies repentant, Iago is held for torture (**ii**).

# THE TRAGEDY OF KING LEAR

## Cast of Characters

### *Main Characters*

LEAR, King of Britain. A hot-tempered, querulous, and selfish old man, Lear displays his lack of realism, first, by dividing his kingdom and, second, by basing his opinion of his daughters on their oral protestations of love for him. However, while spending the night in the storm, he becomes conscious, for the first time in his life, that there are sufferers in the world and that he has in the past taken too little account of this fact. With this first lesson in real humility fresh upon him, he enters his mad stage; and when he recovers from his madness, he is a completely chastened man, one who feels keenly his kinship with humanity and whose selfishness is a thing of the past.

DUKE OF CORNWALL, husband of Regan. Cornwall belongs to the powers of evil in this tragedy. Only his death at the hands of a servant prevents him from being a participant in the war with France and from being liquidated at that time, together with the other evil characters. He backs to the hilt the villainy of Goneril and Regan.

DUKE OF ALBANY, husband of Goneril. At first a seemingly weak character, Albany becomes aroused by the mistreatment of Lear and by the blinding of Gloucester. He fights for Britain because the French have invaded his country, not out of sympathy for the British cause. When he discovers the depths of his wife's infamy, he casts her off; and he remains as one of the men left to clean up the debris left by the powers of evil.

EARL OF KENT. An outspoken and clear-minded man, Kent remains a true friend of Lear throughout the play. Banished because of his plain speaking when Lear cast off Cordelia, he returns disguised to aid the King in his hour of greatest need. In spite of his tactlessness he is almost wholly an admirable figure.

EARL OF GLOUCESTER. A good, if slightly fussy, old man, Gloucester is betrayed by his bastard son, Edmund. His course runs roughly parallel with Lear's, his blindness representing on the physical, or lower, level what Lear's madness represents on the mental and spiritual level. With consummate art, Shakespeare carries on simultaneously the main plot and the Gloucester subplot, and dovetails them through Edmund's enlistment in the forces opposing Lear and Cordelia.

EDGAR, SON OF GLOUCESTER. The conventional "good" son, Edgar remains rather colorless in a gallery of colorful characters. Betrayed by Edmund, he feigns madness and leads his blind father to Dover. After he slays Edmund in single combat, he is one of the men left to rule the devastated kingdom.

EDMUND, bastard son of Gloucester. Shakespeare motivates Edmund's villainy rather carefully. Being a bastard, Edmund cannot share in his father's estates until he rids himself of Edgar. As he sinks deeper and deeper into evil, Edmund directly causes his father's blindness in order to come immediately into his father's estate, makes love in turn to Goneril and Regan, and gives the order for Cordelia's murder. His death at the hand of Edgar serves the cause of poetic justice, and his deathbed repentance helps to clear up certain complications in the plot.

GONERIL, Lear's eldest daughter. Tigerish and conscienceless, Goneril takes the lead in the plots against Lear. She encourages Edmund's advances and plots the death of Albany.

REGAN, Lear's second daughter. Shakespeare carefully discriminates between the characters of Goneril and Regan. As feline and as unscrupulous as Goneril, Regan never seems to have her sister's resolution.

CORDELIA, youngest daughter of Lear. Although she loves her father deeply, Cordelia refuses to pay lipservice to this love. This refusal leads directly to the catastrophe. Had Cordelia convinced Lear of her love, she would not have been exiled and perhaps could have prevented her sisters' villainy. However, although she is tactless, she remains one of Shakespeare's great women. With an almost Roman stoicism, she attempts to repair the wrongs that her sisters have done to her father.

### Supporting Characters

DUKE OF BURGUNDY, refuses Cordelia because of her lack of dowry.

CURAN, a courtier

OSWALD, steward to Goneril

FOOL, one of Shakespeare's great creations. His bitter and shrewd comments to Lear are intended to keep the old King conscious of his rights in the kingdom and of his comparative powerlessness to assume them.

KING OF FRANCE, who, in love with Cordelia, marries her in spite of Lear's displeasure.

(Old Man, tenant to Gloucester; Doctor; a Captain employed by Edmund; Gentleman attendant to Cordelia; a Herald; Servants to Cornwall; Knights of Lear's train; Captains; Messengers; Soldiers; and Attendants)

(Place: *Britain*)

BACKGROUND. The date of composition is probably either late in 1605 or early in 1606. The texts are the first (or "Pied Bull") quarto (1608), a second quarto (either 1608 or 1619) based on the first, and the version in the First Folio (1623). Of these the First Folio text is regarded as the most nearly accurate. The ultimate source is to be found in Geoffrey of Monmouth's *Historia Regum Brittanniae* (c. 1135). It was passed on in Holinshed's Chronicle and John Higgins' *The First parte of the Mirrour for Magistrates*. Spencer used it in the *Faerie Queene*. There was also an anonymous play, *The True Chronicle History of King Leir* (1605).

## ACT BY ACT ANALYSIS

**ACT I.** King Lear, old and tired of the responsibilities of the kingship, announces his intention to divide the Kingdom of Britain among his three daughters. Before the actual division he asks each daughter separately to tell him how much she loves him. The two elder daughters, Goneril and Regan, overflow with protestations of devotion; but Cordelia, who is sickened by the mouthings of her hypocritical sisters, declares that she loves her father according to her bond, "no more nor less." Stung with anger by this apparent unnaturalness in his daughter, Lear casts her off as unworthy. He persists in his determination in spite of the protests of the Earl of Kent, whom Lear banishes for his defense of Cordelia. However, the King of France, who has sued for Cordelia's hand before her disgrace, affirms his intention to marry her in spite of her present lack of dowry. Lear, who is to retain the title of King, now intends to visit Goneril and Regan on alternate months and to be accompanied on his visits by one hundred knights. Goneril and Regan decide privately to consult together and to try to reduce their father's power (i). Consequently, when Lear visits Goneril, she instructs her servants to treat him negligently (iii). However, when Oswald snubs Lear, Kent, who in disguise is back in the King's service, trips him up and strikes him. Immediately Goneril enters and demands that Lear dismiss his knights. Angered by this insult, he decides to cut short his visit and go to Regan. Goneril thereupon sends Oswald with a message to Regan, carrying the news of her quarrel with Lear (iv). Lear sends Kent also with a letter for Regan (v). Meanwhile Edmund, bastard son of the Earl of Gloucester, plots against Edgar, the legitimate heir. He first shows his father a letter, purportedly from Edgar, which suggests that the two boys supersede their father. Edmund then informs Edgar that their father is angry with him and advises him to go armed (ii).

**ACT II.** Edmund now completes his plot against Edgar by pretending to fight him, by smearing himself with blood, and by telling Gloucester that Edgar has sought to enlist him in the murder of their father. At this point Regan and her husband, the Duke of Cornwall, arrive at Gloucester's castle in order to be away from home when Lear arrives there (i). Meanwhile, Kent and Oswald, the two messengers meet. When Kent beats Oswald, Regan and Cornwall consign Kent to the stocks (ii), and Kent is still in the stocks when Lear arrives with his Fool. Lear is left to cool his heels outside Gloucester's castle while Regan and Cornwall take their time in coming out to meet him. When they finally arrive, Lear pours out his grievances against Goneril and demands to know who has stocked his servant, but he meets with scant sympathy. When Goneril arrives on the scene and Lear discovers that Cornwall himself has stocked Kent, the King finally realizes that his two daughters are in league against him. They demand that he follow his original procedure of alternate monthly visits, but that he divest himself completely of his retinue. Almost mad with rage and chagrin, Lear, with Kent and the Fool, withdraws into the night, although a storm is brewing (iv). Meanwhile Edgar, fearing for his life, decides to play mad (iii).

**ACT III.** Kent hears that there has been a division between the Duke of Cornwall and the Duke of Albany, Goneril's husband; and that the King of France and Cordelia have landed at Dover with an army to try to rescue Lear from his persecutors (**i**). Meanwhile, Lear, who is gradually going mad, is standing bareheaded in the storm and defying the elements. Kent decides to lead the group to a hovel which stands nearby (**ii**). At the same time, Gloucester tells Edmund of the division between the Dukes and of France's invasion of England, and suggests that they incline to Lear's party. Edmund now intends to inform Cornwall of his father's defection (**iii**). On the heath Lear and Kent meet first Edgar, who is disguised as Tom o' Bedlam, and then Gloucester, who leads them into the hovel (**iv**). Inside, Lear, aided by Edgar, stages a mock trial of his daughters. Finally Kent and Gloucester get the King to bed, intending to transport him to Cordelia at Dover as soon as possible (**vi**). Meanwhile, Edmund has betrayed his father's intentions to Cornwall (**v**). Consequently, when Gloucester returns to the castle, he is imprisoned by the Duke. Cornwall suggests that Edmund not watch the punishment of his father; Edmund hypocritically agrees. Then, although Cornwall succeeds in blinding Gloucester, the Duke is attacked by a horrified servant, who mortally wounds him (**vii**).

**ACT IV.** Led by an old man, Gloucester meets the disguised Edgar, who intends now to lead his father to Dover and promises to aid him in jumping off a cliff (**i**). Near Dover, Edgar allows Gloucester to roll down a small incline. Gloucester, thinking that he has fallen from a cliff, believes that he has been miraculously saved from death (**vi**). Also at Dover, the mad Lear has refused to see Cordelia (**iii**). However, after he has wandered in the fields (**vi**), he is allowed to sleep. When he awakens, his mind is clear, and he recognizes his daughter (**vii**). Meanwhile Goneril (**ii**) and Regan have both fallen in love with Edmund. Regan is jealous of her sister when she discovers that Oswald carries a letter from Goneril to Edmund (**v**). This letter, which is a declaration of Goneril's contempt for Albany and of her love for Edmund, falls into Edgar's hands when he is forced to kill Oswald, who has attempted to take Gloucester prisoner for the price on his head (**vi**).

**ACT V.** The armies of France and Britain now face one another at Dover. Albany arrives to join his forces with those led by Regan and Edmund. Although Albany feels that Lear's cause is more nearly just than the daughters', he must help defend Britain against a foreign invasion. As Albany muses, Edgar, still disguised, enters, hands him the letter from Goneril to Edmund, and offers to produce a champion should the validity of the letter be called into question. Edmund, who has sworn his love to both sisters, decides to let chance decide which one he shall marry; he also decides that, no matter what else happens, Lear and Cordelia must die (i). Soon after battle begins, the French are defeated (ii); and Lear and Cordelia are taken prisoners. Edmund sends them away under close guard and secretly gives orders for Cordelia's murder. When Albany appears, he arrests Edmund for high treason and offers to prove it in combat if no other champion can be found. The Herald calls for the champion; and Edgar appears, fights with and mortally wounds his brother. Then he reveals himself to Edmund and informs the company that Gloucester is dead. Meanwhile, Goneril has poisoned Regan and stabbed herself. In the confusion everyone has forgotten Lear and Cordelia, when suddenly Edmund suggests that if Cordelia's life is to be saved, a message must be sent immediately. However, help arrives too late; and Lear enters carrying his dead daughter. Lear himself then dies of grief. When Albany suggests that Edgar and Kent rule the realm, Kent, feeling death upon him, refuses. Edgar and Albany must now restore order in the state (iii).

# THE TRAGEDY OF MACBETH

## Cast of Characters

### *Main Characters*

DUNCAN, King of Scotland, evidently a mild-mannered King, murdered by Macbeth and Lady Macbeth.

MALCOLM, son of Duncan. When Duncan is murdered, Malcolm, fearful of meeting the same fate, flies to England. There Macduff beseeches him to come back to Scotland and claim his throne. His army of English and rebel Scots defeat and kill Macbeth. Malcolm is then King of Scotland.

MACBETH, General of the King's army, afterwards King of Scotland. Macbeth is a complex character: imaginative and sensitive, he recoils at first from the murder of Duncan, even though he is ambitious to become King. Under the prodding of his wife he does the deed; then after he wears the crown, he begins to understand that crime begets crime. Fearful on his shaky throne, he commits murder after murder, until the Scottish thanes revolt and depose him. The influence of the Weird Sisters on him is problematical; probably to Shakespeare they represented objectified witches, but the title *weird* applied to them ties them up with the old Anglo-Saxon conception of a man's *wyrd* or fate.

BANQUO, General of the King's army. Banquo acts as a foil for Macbeth. The witches predict that Banquo's issue will be kings, but Banquo does not lift a finger to hasten the day. He is murdered by Macbeth, (1) because Macbeth realizes that Banquo suspects him of the murder of Duncan, (2) because the witches have predicted that Banquo's issue rather than Macbeth's will rule Scotland. In the old chronicle Banquo joins with Macbeth to murder the King; however, since James I of England was proud of his descent from Banquo, Shakespeare probably changed Banquo's character for reasons of policy.

MACDUFF, Macbeth's special nemesis. Since Macduff has been born without the labor of his mother, he can circumvent the prophecy made to Macbeth by the witches.

LADY MACBETH, wife to Macbeth. She has often been played as a villainess par excellence. Certainly she seems more resolute and bloodthirsty than her husband in the early stages of the play. However, all her ambition seems to be for Macbeth rather than for herself; she steels him to do what he really wants to do. Further, her sleepwalking scene in Act V shows her as possessing a conscience. She is there undergoing penance for her misdeeds. Shakespeare does not show her as Macbeth's partner in crime after the murder of Duncan, and she does not even appear in Act IV when Macbeth is undergoing his greatest degeneration.

### Supporting Characters

ANGUS, Scottish noble

CAITHNESS, Scottish noble

DONALBAIN, younger son of Duncan

FLEANCE, Banquo's son, who manages to escape his father's fate

HECATE

LENNOX, Scottish noble

LADY MACDUFF, killed by order of Macbeth

MENTEITH, Scottish noble

ROSS, Scottish noble

SEYTON, an officer attending Macbeth

SIWARD, Earl of Northumberland

YOUNG SIWARD, Northumberland's son

THREE WITCHES, the weird sisters

> (Gentlewoman; an old man; an English doctor and a Scotch doctor; Captain; a drunken porter; Boy, son of Macduff; Apparitions, Lords, Gentlemen, Officers, Soldiers, Murderers, Attendants, and Messengers)

(Place: *Scotland and England*)

BACKGROUND. The probable date of composition is 1606. The only text is to be found in the First Folio (1623), a version which many scholars believe to be garbled. Undoubtedly there are interpolations by other playwrights in this version—perhaps principally by Middleton. The source is Holinshed's *Chronicle*.

## ACT BY ACT ANALYSIS

**ACT I.** Duncan, King of Scotland, has found it necessary to meet two threats to his kingdom. The first, a rebellion led by Macdonwald, has been put down by Duncan's great generals, Macbeth and Banquo. Then when the Norwegians, taking advantage of the rebellion, launched an attack on Scotland, Macbeth has met this threat; and in defeating the Norwegians, he has captured the Thane of Cawdor, who is an ally of the Norwegians. Duncan bestows this rebel's title *in absentia* on Macbeth, and orders Ross to greet Macbeth as Thane of Cawdor (**ii**). Meanwhile, Macbeth and Banquo, returning from the wars, meet three witches who hail Macbeth first as Thane of Glamis, next as Thane of Cawdor, and finally as one "that shalt be King hereafter." When Macbeth is startled by this prophecy, they turn to Banquo and prophesy that he shall beget kings though he be none. Macbeth already has the title of Thane of Glamis; and when Ross appears and calls him Thane of Cawdor, Macbeth's ambition begins to grow (**iii**). When Macbeth and Banquo meet Duncan, the King asserts his intention of passing the night in Macbeth's castle at Inverness. Duncan then proclaims Malcolm Prince of Cumberland and heir to the throne (**iv**). At Inverness, Lady Macbeth, who has received all the developments in a letter from her husband (**v**), subtly reinforces Macbeth's half-expressed notion of murdering Duncan while the King remains at Inverness (**vi**). Macbeth, although he realizes that there are many reasons why he should not murder Duncan, under prodding from his wife determines to commit the crime (**vii**).

**ACT II.** Banquo refuses to be tempted to hasten the fulfillment of the prophecy (**i**). But Macbeth and his wife go ahead with plans for the murder. After Lady Macbeth has drugged the King's servants, whom she plans to blame for the crime, Macbeth enters Duncan's chamber and stabs the King. However, when he refuses to re-enter the chamber to smear the servants with Duncan's blood, his wife undertakes the task. Then when they hear a knocking at the door, they both retire to wash off the blood (**ii**). This knocking has come from Macduff and Lennox, who have traveled here to meet the King. When they are admitted, they discover the murder. The blame is immediately laid on the servants; and Macbeth kills them, ostensibly to avenge the murder, but actually to shut their mouths. Malcolm and Donalbain, to avoid meeting their father's fate, decide to fly from Scotland: Malcolm to England and Donalbain to Ireland (**iii**). Because of their hasty flight, they are believed to be accomplices in the murder; and Macbeth is chosen King (**iv**).

**ACT III.** Macbeth now is driven to plot the murder of Banquo, who suspects foul play, and Fleance; for in accordance with the witches' prophecy, Macbeth must rid himself of Banquo's line to assure the kingship for his own heirs. He dissembles and ironically invites Banquo to attend a state dinner (**i**). Although Lady Macbeth half suspects her husband's intentions, Macbeth will tell her none of his plans for the murder of Banquo (**ii**). Macbeth's hired murderers succeed in murdering Banquo, but Fleance escapes (**iii**). Then, at the banquet given by Macbeth for his retainers, the ghost of Banquo appears, visible only to Macbeth, and appropriates the King's chair. Driven almost to distraction by this apparition, Macbeth talks wildly; and the banquet breaks up in disorder (**iv**). Meanwhile Macduff, who has evidently suspected Macbeth of duplicity, has gone to England, in an attempt to arouse Malcolm to return to Scotland and claim the throne (**vi**).

**ACT IV.** Macbeth, worried by the desertion of a number of his subjects, revisits the Weird Sisters. He receives from them three prophecies: (1) that he must beware of Macduff, (2) that "none of woman born shall harm" him, and (3) that he shall never be vanquished until Birnam Wood comes to Dunsinane. Finally they show him a line of kings descended from Banquo. When Macbeth then hears that Macduff has fled to England, he plans to kill all of Macduff's family (**i**). Macbeth immediately pursues this plan and sends murderers to dispose of Macduff's wife and children (**ii**). Meanwhile, in England, Macduff succeeds in getting Malcolm's consent to lead English troops into Scotland and to claim the throne. Before he consents, Malcolm, suspecting Macduff is an agent of Macbeth, tests him thoroughly (**iii**).

**ACT V.** At Dunsinane Lady Macbeth has taken to sleepwalking, a sign that her mind is deteriorating. As she walks, she re-enacts her crimes and thus reveals to onlookers the depth of her sins (**i**). Meanwhile, a number of Scottish thanes mean to desert to the English army, which is marching on Scotland, led by Malcolm and Siward (**ii**). When the groups join, Malcolm orders the troops each to hew down a bough from Birnam Wood and hold it before him to conceal the size of the army (**iv**). Macbeth has been taking comfort from the prophecies of the witches (**iii**), but when he hears that the woods seem to be marching against Dunsinane, he loses much of his confidence. Meanwhile, he hears that his wife has died, presumably a suicide (**v**). Before the castle the battle is joined (**vi**). Macbeth engages in combat with young Siward and kills the youth (**vii**); but when he meets Macduff and warns him that no man born of woman can harm Macbeth, Macduff contemptuously replies that he has been "from his mother's womb untimely ripp'd." Despairingly but bravely, Macbeth hurls a challenge at his adversary, and they leave the stage fighting. When Macduff re-enters with Macbeth's head, Malcolm is proclaimed King. The new King raises to the rank of earl all the thanes who have helped him, and promises to rule Scotland justly and well (**viii**).

# ANTONY AND CLEOPATRA

## Cast of Characters

### *Main Characters*

CLEOPATRA, beautiful, tempestuous queen of Egypt, from whose charms Antony is unable to escape

MARK ANTONY, one of the three triumvirs or rulers of Rome, is so blinded by his love for Cleopatra that he loses his warrior's judgment and dissipates his powers carousing with his beloved in Egypt.

OCTAVIUS CAESAR, triumvir of Rome, is hard, cold, and calculating. His victory over Antony is brought about more by Antony's weakness than by Caesar's strength.

M. AEMILIUS LEPIDUS, the third and weakest triumvir, is used by Caesar as he had earlier been used by Mark Antony (See *Julius Caesar*).

SEXTUS POMPEIUS (POMPEY), a hot-headed young naval leader whose rebellion finally draws Antony back from Egypt

DOMITIUS ENOBARBUS, shrewd and cynical follower, is finally driven by his opportunism to desert his master.

OCTAVIA, Caesar's sister, is a cool, quiet woman (the opposite of Cleopatra), who marries Antony in an attempt to cement friendship between Antony and Caesar.

### *Supporting Characters*

AGRIPPA, follower of Caesar

ALEXAS, attendant on Cleopatra

CANIDIUS, Antony's lieutenant general

CHARMIAN, attendant on Cleopatra

DEMETRIUS, follower of Antony

DERCETAS, follower of Antony

DIOMEDES, attendant on Cleopatra
DOLABELLA, follower of Caesar
EROS, follower of Antony
EUPHRONIUS, a schoolmaster-ambassador
GALLUS, follower of Caesar
IRAS, attendant on Cleopatra
MAECENAS, follower of Caesar
MARDIAN, attendant on Cleopatra
MENAS, follower of Pompey
MENECRATES, follower of Pompey
PHILO, follower of Antony
PROCULEIUS, follower of Caesar
SCARUS, follower of Antony
SELEUCUS, attendant on Cleopatra
SILIUS, an officer serving Ventidius
TAURUS, Caesar's lieutenant general
THYREUS, follower of Caesar
VARRIUS, follower of Pompey
VENTIDIUS, follower of Antony

(A Soothsayer, a Clown, Officers, Soldiers, Messengers, and Attendants)

(Place: *In different parts of the Roman Empire*)

BACKGROUND. This play was probably composed about 1607. As in *Julius Caesar*, Shakespeare's source is Thomas North's translation of Plutarch's *Lives*. Though he follows his source faithfully, he juggles the chronology for greater dramatic effect. Thus Shakespeare omits Antony's long struggle with the Parthians, makes no mention of the children of Antony and Octavia, shortens Antony's stay in Rome from a period of years to one of weeks, and says nothing about Octavia's conquest of Antony, who (according to Plutarch) remained faithful to her for years. Shakespeare's chief contribution to the story, however, is the subtle tones with which he draws the characters of Antony and Cleopatra in contrast to Plutarch's blunt, straightforward delineation.

## ACT BY ACT ANALYSIS

**ACT I.** Antony's followers sorrowfully watch their once mighty leader carouse in Alexandria, held there by his passion for the beautiful Cleopatra (i). A messenger from Rome, who finally gains admittance to Antony, brings word that his wife, Fulvia, is dead, and that Rome is torn by unrest and unsettled by the revolt of young Pompey. Antony is conscience-stricken and prepares to leave for Rome at once (ii). Cleopatra attempts to dissuade him; but, seeing that his mind is made up, she changes her tactics and urges him to go (iii), though when he leaves she keeps a score of messengers busily engaged carrying information between her and her beloved (v). In Rome, meanwhile, Caesar condemns Antony for his neglect of duty, while Lepidus tries his best to smooth away Caesar's anger (iv).

**ACT II.** While Pompey wonders how Antony's return will affect his revolt (i), Enobarbus and Lepidus try to soothe the injured feelings of Caesar and Antony, who quarrel furiously the moment they meet. At an opportune time Agrippa (one of Caesar's followers) suggests that, since Antony is now a widower, a marriage be arranged between him and Octavia, Caesar's sister. Such a marriage would insure continued friendship between the quarreling triumvirs. Caesar agrees and so, surprisingly, does Antony, though Enobarbus privately predicts that Antony will never leave Cleopatra (ii). When Cleopatra hears of the marriage, she rages. After threatening to kill the messenger, she sends her servants to bring her a description of her rival (v). Antony, meanwhile, has been warned by a soothsayer to return to Egypt. Remaining in Rome, the seer says, will only further Caesar's fortunes. Antony admits privately that his marriage to Octavia is one of convenience and that he still is drawn to Cleopatra. He sends one of his lieutenants, Ventidius, to overthrow the Parthians, and plans to return to Egypt as soon as possible (iii). Caesar's military leaders leave Rome to meet Pompey's forces at Mount Misenum (iv). When the generals meet, Caesar parleys with Pompey, who (fearing Antony's might will be aligned with Caesar's) agrees to the terms. Enobarbus, though, again predicts that Antony will never leave Cleopatra (vi). In the drunken feast aboard Pompey's galley that follows the truce, Pompey refuses to take advantage of his former enemies (vii).

**ACT III.** While Antony's eastern campaign is progressing successfully under Ventidius (i), Caesar and Antony follow Antony's marriage with an oath of friendship, though Caesar still has some misgivings (**ii**). In Alexandria, Cleopatra hears a disparaging description of Octavia and is sure her lover will return to her (**iii**). Her prediction seems strengthened when Antony tells his new bride that he is again angry with Caesar, and that he plans to make war against his brother-in-law. As for Octavia, Antony tells her that she must choose between him and her brother (**iv**). Unable to give up her brother, she returns to Caesar. She finds that Antony is already in Egypt raising an army (**vi**). It is reported, too, that Caesar (feeling no further need for Lepidus' support) has turned against his fellow triumvir (**v**). Antony, in Egypt, to the despair of his military leaders, listens to Cleopatra's advice and plans to meet Caesar's forces on the sea instead of on the land (**vii**). The wily Caesar plans to hold his land army in check until the sea battle will have ended (**viii**), while Antony instructs Enobarbus to place his troops so that he can see the number and disposition of Caesar's ships (**ix**). When the fleets meet, Antony's cowardly Egyptian admiral flees and his ships are devastated. Antony's general Canidius immediately plans to desert to Caesar, but Enobarbus remains steadfast (**x**). Antony blames Cleopatra for his defeat and all seems lost (**xi**). He sends an ambassador to sue for peace with Caesar. He asks that Cleopatra be left with Egypt's crown and that he be allowed to remain in Egypt or to live in Athens as a private citizen. Caesar scorns his request. Cleopatra's desires will be granted only if she will agree to drive Antony from Egypt or to kill him. Caesar sends Thyreus to Cleopatra with orders to promise her anything in order to win her from Antony (**xii**). Antony, who intercepts Thyreus, has him whipped and sends back a challenge to Caesar to meet him in single combat. This done, Antony, who believes the tides of war have once more turned in his favor plans one more orgy before the final battle. Enobarbus sadly watches his master deteriorate. In order to save himself, he decides that he must at last desert to Caesar (**xiii**).

**ACT IV.** Caesar laughs at Antony's challenge. With the aid of the troops who have deserted Antony, he has more than enough strength to meet his enemy (**i**). Faced with Caesar's refusal, Antony has strange forebodings. He pledges his followers to win or to die on the morrow (**ii**). These forebodings

seem strengthened when superstitious soldiers, hearing noises
in the streets, believe they hear the god Hercules deserting
Antony (**iii**). After his last night of revelry, Antony is preparing himself for battle (**iv**), when he hears the crushing news
that Enobarbus has deserted. Far from blaming him, Antony
orders all the general's treasures sent after him, together with
kind letters (**v**). When Enobarbus hears of this kindly action
(**vi**), he is almost beside himself and dies of a broken heart(**ix**).
At first the battle goes well for Antony. He defeats those sent
against him (**vii**), and drives his enemies back to their own camp
(**viii**). Again convinced that Caesar's forces are weakest at sea,
Antony plans a second sea battle (**x**). But Caesar, seeing
Antony's naval strength, plans to attack by land (**xi**). As before,
Antony's Egyptian fleet flees. Raging, Antony again blames
Cleopatra (**xii**). Fearing for her life, the Queen hides in a
monument and has her women take word to Antony that she is
dead (**xiii**). When Antony receives this message he orders a
follower to kill him. This order refused, he falls on his sword.
Dying, he learns of Cleopatra's ruse, asks to be carried to her
(**xiv**), and dies in her arms (**xv**).

**ACT V.** Caesar, informed of Antony's death, is saddened. He
sends a messenger to Cleopatra, telling her she shall be treated
gently (**i**); but while Proculeus is delivering the message,
members of the guard enter the monument and capture her.
Though Caesar treats her kindly, her rebellious spirit will not
humble itself. Her crown upon her head, she places a poisonous
asp upon her arm and another upon her bosom. When he finds
the Queen is dead, Caesar says she will be buried with Antony
(**ii**).

# THE LIFE OF TIMON OF ATHENS

## Cast of Characters

### *Main Characters*

TIMON, an overly generous lord, finds that his friends leave when his money runs out, and he turns bitterly against all mankind.

ALCIBIADES, a soldier, fights back from his banishment and conquers his banishers.

FLAVIUS, Timon's steward and his only true friend

APEMANTUS, a bitter, snarling misanthrope

LUCIUS
LUCULLUS  } accept Timon's generosity but refuse to help him
SEMPRONIUS   when he needs money.
VENTIDIUS

### *Supporting Characters*

| | |
|---|---|
| AMAZONS, dancers | LUCIUS, money lender's servant |
| CAPHIS, a servant | PHILOTUS, money lender's servant |
| FLAMINIUS, Timon's servant | |
| HORTENSIUS, money lender's servant | PHRYNIA, Alcibiades' mistress |
| | SERVILIUS, Timon's servant |
| LUCILIUS, Timon's servant | TIMANDRA, Alcibiades' mistress |
| | TITUS, money lender's servant |

(Attendants, Cupid, Bandits, a Fool, a Jeweler, Lords, a Merchant, Officers, an Old Athenian, a Page, a Painter, a Poet, Senators, Soldiers, Strangers, Servants)

(Place: *Athens, and the neighboring woods*)

BACKGROUND. No record exists to show whether this play was ever printed or even produced during Shakespeare's lifetime. Its first printed edition is that of the First Folio (1623). The primary sources of the play are found in various sections of Plutarch's *Lives,* a work familiar to Shakespeare in Sir Thomas North's translation. Additional material is drawn from Lucian's *Timon, or the Misanthrope.* The authorship of the play has been much questioned. It is generally thought to be partly done by another hand than Shakespeare's or to be an older play merely retouched by him.

## ACT BY ACT ANALYSIS

**ACT I.** Timon, acting with his usual generosity, illustrates his good nature by relieving an acquaintance, Ventidius, from debt, and by arranging a marriage for his servant, Lucilius (i). He continues to bestow his patrimony despite the mutterings of surly Apemantus and the pleading of Flavius, his steward, who alone realizes that Timon's treasury is empty (ii).

**ACT II.** Others are also realizing Timon's insolvency. A senator laments Timon's squanderings and sends a servant to collect money owed him (i). The senator is but one of many creditors now descending in a storm upon Timon. But the Athenian lord is not worried. Believing that he is "rich in friends," he sends the steward Flavius to ask for money from these friends to settle his accounts (ii).

**ACT III.** Flavius' request is rejected first by Lucullus, who offers the steward a bribe to tell Timon he has not found Lucullus at home (i). Lucius likewise refuses Flavius (ii), while Sempronius denies him on the grounds that his feelings are hurt because Timon did not approach him first (iii). Fighting off the swarm of creditors at home, Timon bids his servants summon his false friends again. "Once more," he says, "I'll feast the rascals" (iv). When the guests arrive, the banquet dishes are uncovered and found to be full of warm water. To this "feast" Timon adds curses and drives the lords away (vi). Previous to this, Alcibiades, a soldier, who has been refused a request by the senate, has been banished from Athens for his harsh words against that body (v).

**ACT IV.** Timon, in an agony of rage against his false friends, screams out a curse against all Athens (i), while his servants meet with the steward Flavius to share his small savings and to lament Timon's ruin (ii). Timon flees to a cave in the woods. While digging roots to eat, he finds a hoard of buried gold. Alcibiades (together with his mistresses, Phrynia and Timandra) comes to Timon's lonely cave accompanied by a band of soldiers. He tells Timon of a plan to sack Athens. Timon abuses all his guests but gives the women gold for themselves and Alcibiades gold to pay his followers, who are deserting for lack of pay. Apemantus visits Timon and receives like abuse. A robber band comes through the forest, and Timon gives them gold freely. Last in this procession of visitors is Flavius, who comes to plead with Timon; but his lord will not recognize him and sends him away with yet more gold (**iii**).

**ACT V.** The rumor that Timon still has gold circulates rapidly, as does the story that his bankruptcy was merely a pretense to test his friends. A poet and a painter seek him out, but he drives them away. The Athenian senators, now frightened by Alcibiades' approaching army, send Flavius with representatives to plead with Timon to lead them against the banished soldier's forces. Despite their promises of honors and riches, Timon drives them away (**i**). Back in Athens the senate's deputation has just brought the news that Timon will not help them (**ii**), when a soldier enters with the news that he has just discovered Timon's dead body in his lonely cave (**iii**). Their last hope for leadership gone, the senators admit the conquering Alcibiades without a struggle. The soldier pardons all except his own enemies and the false friends of Timon. These he promises to punish (**iv**).

# THE TRAGEDY OF CORIOLANUS

## Cast of Characters

### *Main Characters*

CAIUS MARCIUS, afterwards Caius Marcius Coriolanus. The tragedy of Coriolanus is the tragedy of a proud, stiff-necked, valiant warrior who is unable to meet the exigencies of politics or to recognize the necessity of being tactful. Trained by his mother to be a warrior, Coriolanus in a military sense is more than once the savior of Rome; however, his contempt for the plebeians, for their spokesmen, and, in a sense, for all civil authority, leads to his downfall.

MENENIUS AGRIPPA, friend of Coriolanus. Menenius, although a rather gossipy old man, recognizes what Coriolanus fails to realize: a man must sometimes yield to custom with a good grace, and military prowess is not the sole qualification for civil leadership.

TULLUS AUFIDIUS, general of the Volscians. Aufidius is a great military leader, but in contrast to Coriolanus he is a realist. Although an enemy of Coriolanus, he receives the Roman renegade with open arms, only to become jealous of Corialanus' popularity and to plot and carry out his murder.

VOLUMNIA, mother of Coriolanus. In Volumnia, Shakespeare has created the traditional Roman matron: stern, unbending, martial—training her son to be nothing more than a warrior. She has cause afterwards to regret the complete success of her handiwork when she realizes that Coriolanus has no conception of civil duty.

VIRGILIA, wife of Coriolanus. A sweet and retiring woman, Virgilia acts as a foil for Volumnia.

### *Supporting Characters*

TITUS LARTIUS  
COMINIUS } generals against the Volscians. They are always ready to give full credit to Coriolanus for his military success.

SICINUS VELUTUS ⎫   tribunes of the people. Clever and subtle,
                ⎪   these tribunes constantly needle Coriolanus
                ⎬   into losing his temper and making rash state-
                ⎪   ments. Eventually they are responsible for his
JUNIUS BRUTUS   ⎭   banishment from Rome.

YOUNG MARCIUS, son of Coriolanus

VALERIA, friend to Virgilia

   (A Roman Herald; Aufidius' lieutenant; Conspirators with
   Aufidius; A Citizen of Antium; Two Volscian Guards;
   Gentlewoman, attending on Virgilia; Roman and Volscian
   Senators; Patricians; Aediles; Lictors; Soldiers; Citizens;
   Messengers; Servants to Aufidius; and other Attendants)

   (Place:  *Rome and the neighborhood; Carioli and the
   neighborhood; Antium*)

BACKGROUND. The date of composition is either late in 1608 or
early in 1609. The only text is the one in the First Folio (1623).
The source is Sir Thomas North's translation of Plutarch's *Life of
Coriolanus*.

## ACT BY ACT ANALYSIS

**ACT I.** The plebeians of Rome have revolted against the
patricians because they lack food. The common people believe
that the patricians are hoarding corn for their own use.
Menenius Agrippa insists to a group of citizens that the
patricians are doing all within their power to provide food for
Rome and reasonably asks them to be patient. However, when
Caius Marcius, the great warrior of Rome, appears he bitterly
scolds the rabble. He reports angrily that the patricians, to
avert the revolt, have consented to the appointment of five
plebeian tribunes to represent the people; two of the five are
Junius Brutus and Sicinius Velutus. At this point, word comes
that the Volscians are in arms under the leadership of Tullus
Aufidius, Caius Marcius' hated, yet respected, enemy. Caius
Marcius is immediately called to action with the Roman army,
under the leadership of Cominius and Titus Lartius (**i**). He
goes with the blessing of his mother, Volumnia, who has reared
him to be a warrior (**iii**). Meanwhile, Aufidius prepares himself
to meet Caius Marcius, who has defeated him several times in
single combat (**ii**). At Carioli, the battle is joined. At first,
the battle goes against the Romans under Titus Lartius; but
singlehanded Caius Marcius rallies the army (**iv**), and the

Romans capture the city (**v**). Although severely wounded, Caius Marcius joins the other Roman army still outside the city, and looks for Aufidius (**vi**). When Aufidius and Caius Marcius meet, the Roman again defeats his adversary; but Aufidius is rescued by some of his men (**viii**). The city completely reduced, the two Roman armies join forces; and Caius Marcius is given the name Coriolanus because of his feats at Carioli (**ix**).

**ACT II.** Back in Rome, Coriolanus is nominated for consul by the patricians; to obtain the honor, however, he must stand in the market place, show his wounds to the plebeians, and ask for their votes. Recognizing Coriolanus' contempt for the plebeians, Brutus and Sicinius decide to egg the warrior into insulting the citizens, since they fear they will lose influence should Coriolanus become consul. Meanwhile, on his return to Rome, Coriolanus is met by Volumnia and an admiring group of patricians and plebeians (**i**). In spite of Coriolanus' reluctance to stand in the market place, the Senators convince him that he must do so to obtain the consulship (**ii**). In the Forum, Coriolanus disdainfully asks for the votes of a number of citizens. At first, they are inclined to give him their votes; but after he leaves, Brutus and Sicinius persuade them to change their minds and to refuse him the consulship (**iii**).

**ACT III.** When the two tribunes meet Coriolanus, they inform him of the citizens' decision and needle him into such rash statements .that they seem justified in having him arrested for treason. Coriolanus and the other gentry, however, force the tribunes and the citizens to retire. The tribunes then return with reinforcements and demand that the patricians relinquish Coriolanus for punishment (**i**). Meanwhile, at home, Coriolanus hears entreaties from Volumnia, Menenius, and Cominius that he give himself up and apologize to the citizens. Reluctantly, he prepares to return to the Forum (**ii**). In the Forum, Coriolanus begins his apology; but again needled by the tribunes, he loses his temper and speaks rashly. Immediately he is sentenced to banishment from Rome. He leaves the Forum, pursued by the jeers of the citizenry (**iii**).

**ACT IV.** Before one of the gates of Rome, Coriolanus says his farewells to his friends (**i**), while the tribunes enjoy their moment of victory over their old enemy (**ii**). Coriolanus repairs in disguise to Antium, obtains an audience with Aufidius, and offers to join forces with the Volscians. In spite of his former hatred of Coriolanus, Aufidius welcomes him, and the two plan to attack Rome (**v**). Meanwhile in Rome the gloating of Sicinius and Brutus and the rejoicing of the citizens turn to fear when they hear that Coriolanus and Aufidius are marching on Rome (**vi**). Although Aufidius is happy to have Coriolanus' aid in the enterprise, the great popularity of Coriolanus with the Volscian soldiers is beginning to awaken Aufidius' envy; Aufidius decides, however, to postpone any vengeance against Coriolanus until Rome is taken (**vii**).

**ACT V.** The Volscians being everywhere victorious, Cominius goes to Coriolanus in the Volscian camp and begs him not to invade Rome. Meeting with no success in his venture, Cominius joins with other Romans in requesting Menenius to try to soften Coriolanus (**i**). Coriolanus, however, refuses to see his old friend (**ii**), since he has promised Aufidius not to communicate with Romans. The next ambassadors sent by the Romans to Coriolanus consist of his mother, his wife, and his son. Unable to withstand their united entreaties, he promises to spare Rome (**iii**). This news is received in Rome with great rejoicing (**iv, v**); but when Coriolanus returns to Carioli, Aufidius plans to have him murdered on the pretext that Coriolanus has betrayed the Volscians. As Coriolanus appears, followed by an admiring mob, the conspirators murder him. Aufidius publicly assumes responsibility for and defends the murder, though he half repents the deed (**vi**).

# INDEX